T E S T

Your Quranic Knowledge

EDIP YUKSEL

Brainbow Press
Hundred Fourteen Books

> www.19.org
> www.yuksel.org
> www.quranix.com
> www.islamicreform.org
> www.brainbowpress.com

ISBN 978-0-9796715-5-5

ISBN: 978-0-9796715-5-5

5 0 7 9 5

9 780979 671555

Cover Design: Uğur Şahin

Printed in the United States of America

10 9 8 7 6 5 4 3

EDIP YUKSEL is an American-Turkish-Kurdish author and activist who spent four years in Turkish prisons in the 1980's for his political writings and activities promoting an Islamic revolution in Turkey. He experienced a paradigm change in 1986 transforming him from a Sunni religion to *islam*, surrendering to God alone, peacemaking or rational monotheism. Edip Yüksel has written more than twenty books and hundreds of articles on religion, politics, philosophy and law in Turkish, and numerous articles and books in English. Edip is the founder of 19.org, the Islamic Reform organization, and co-founder of Muslims for Peace Justice and Progress (MPJP). His personal site is yuksel.org. After receiving his bachelor degrees from the University of Arizona in Philosophy and Near Eastern Studies, Edip received his law degree from the same university. Edip is an Adjunct Philosophy professor at Pima Community College, and teaches various classes at Accelerated Learning Lab. He is fluent in Turkish, English and Classic Arabic; proficient in Persian, and barely conversant in Kurdish, his mother tongue.

Join the Movement; Let the World Know!

The Islamic Reform movement is receiving momentum around the globe. We invite you to join us in our activities locally, internationally. Please contact us through the contact addresses posted at:

www.islamicreform.org
www.free-minds.org
www.yuksel.org
www.mpjp.org
www.19.org

To study the Quran more diligently, you may visit 19.org for links to computer programs, searchable Quranic indexes, electronic versions of this and other translations, and various study tools. We highly recommend you the following sites for your study of the Quran:

www.quranic.org
www.quranix.com
www.openquran.org
www.studyquran.org
www.quranmiracles.org
www.quranconnection.com

www.19.org	www.yuksel.org	www.free-minds.org	www.islamicreform.org	www.quranmiracles.org	www.brainbowpress.com	www.deenresearchcenter.com	www.quranconnection.com	www.commondreams.org	www.quranbrowser.com	www.openburhan.com	www.studyquran.org	www.quranix.com	www.mpjp.org

Why and How?

Quran, the final testament, orders us to read and study God's message. *Ilm* (Knowledge) and *Hikma* (Wisdom) are the names used frequently for the Quran. Wisdom and knowledge are the most important gifts from God. So, whoever attains wisdom has attained a great bounty (2:269).

Monotheists are encouraged to seek knowledge. But this does not mean that all monotheists are knowledgeable. There are many colors between red and purple. Since Muslims need experts and knowledgeable people (3:7; 4:83), they have to educate some members on God's system (9:122). The importance of knowledge has been stressed many times in Quran (35:28; 39:9). Ignorance gives birth to fanaticism, jealousy, and arrogance and eventually leading to idolatry.

There is more than one reason for preparing this test:

* You may check the level of your Quranic knowledge.
* You may acquire new knowledge or modify some.
* You may learn to study more attentively.
* You may enjoy the Quranic studies more than before.
* You may improve your skills in how to read between the lines, how to infer information, and how to draw conclusions from the verses of Quran.

How to evaluate your test?

For each question there are four answers. You have to choose the best answer and mark it for each question. For each test (20 questions) you have maximum 20 minutes. At the end of the booklet you will find the answer key for all the tests. After each test, count the number of the correct answers and multiply them by five. The result will give your score over a hundred. For example, if your correct answers in the first test are 17, your score is 17x5 = 85. To calculate your average score, you should add all the scores you got from all the tests, and then divide the sum by the number of tests you have taken.

After finishing the first 5 (FIVE) tests, if you wish to get detailed information about your knowledge of the Quran in various fields, you may apply the following rules:

To score your general knowledge about the Quran:

> Count the number of your correct answers from 1 to 6 inclusively in each test, and then multiply the total by 3.3. For instance, if your total correct answers for the questions between 1 and 6 (included) are 25; your score over a hundred is 25x3.3 = 82.5

To score your knowledge about the Quranic history:

> Count the number of your correct answers from 7 to 10 inclusively in each test, and then multiply the total by 5. For instance, if your total correct answers for the questions between 7 and 10 (both included) are 18; your score over a hundred is 18x5 = 90.

To score your knowledge about the mathematical miracle:

> Count the number of your correct answers from 11 to 12 inclusively in each test, and then multiply the total by 10. For instance, if your total correct answers for the questions between 11 and 12 (both included) are 8; your score over a hundred is 8x10=80.

To score your critical reading and understanding level of the Quran:

> Count the number of your correct answers from 13 to 20 inclusively in each test, and then multiply the total by 2.5. For instance, if your total correct answers for the questions between 13 and 20 (both included) are 38; your score is 38x2.5 = 95.

PS:

For the translations of the verses, Quran: a Reformist Translation is used.

20:114	Then high above all is **God**, the King, and the True. Do not be hasty with the Quran before its inspiration is completed to you, and say, "My Lord, increase my knowledge."
7:52	We have brought them a book which We have detailed with knowledge; a guide and a mercy to those who acknowledge.
12:77	They said, "If he has stolen, there was a brother of his before who also had stolen." Joseph kept this all inside himself, and did not reveal anything to them. He said, "You are in a worse position, and **God** best knows what you describe."
29:50	They said, "If only signs would come down to him from his Lord!" Say, "All signs are with **God**, and I am but a clear warner."
2:269	He grants wisdom to whom He chooses, and whoever is granted wisdom, has been given much good. Only those with intelligence will take heed.
16:125	Invite to the path of your Lord with wisdom and good advice, and argue with them in the best possible manner. Your Lord is fully aware of who is misguided from His path, and He is fully aware of the guided ones.

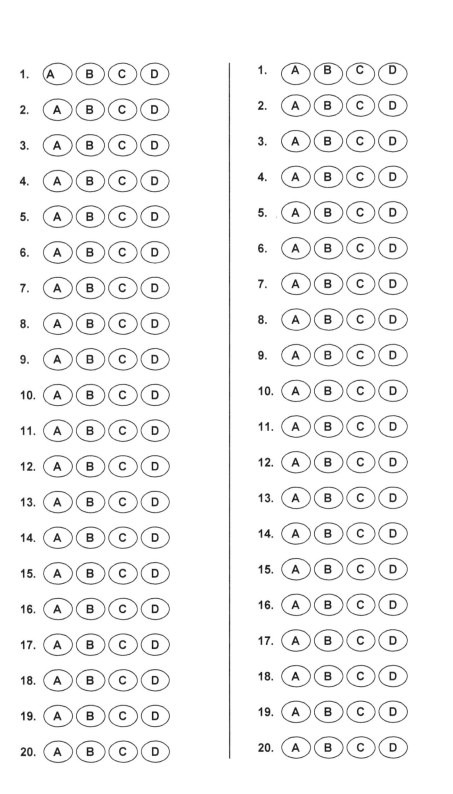

1. A B C D		1. A B C D
2. A B C D		2. A B C D
3. A B C D		3. A B C D
4. A B C D		4. A B C D
5. A B C D		5. A B C D
6. A B C D		6. A B C D
7. A B C D		7. A B C D
8. A B C D		8. A B C D
9. A B C D		9. A B C D
10. A B C D		10. A B C D
11. A B C D		11. A B C D
12. A B C D		12. A B C D
13. A B C D		13. A B C D
14. A B C D		14. A B C D
15. A B C D		15. A B C D
16. A B C D		16. A B C D
17. A B C D		17. A B C D
18. A B C D		18. A B C D
19. A B C D		19. A B C D
20. A B C D		20. A B C D

Test 1

1. Who made the following prayer: "He said, 'My Lord, forgive me, and grant me a kingship that will never be attained by anyone after me. You are the Grantor.'"
    a. Jonah
    b. Jesus
    c. Qarun
    d. Solomon

2. Fill in the space in the following verse: "**God** does not forgive ...., but He forgives other than that for whom He pleases."
    a. to have partners set up with Him
    b. committing adultery
    c. lying
    d. committing murder

3. Fill in the space in the following verse: "the people who truly reverence God are the .... "
    a. charitable
    b. submitter
    c. knowledgeable
    d. poor

4. Which verse talks about a messenger coming after all the prophets?
    a. 3:18
    b. 3:81
    c. 33:7
    d. 57:26

5. Which Chapter has the word "God" in its all verses?
    a. Chapter 60, conventionally called The Test
    b. Chapter 61, conventionally called The Column
    c. Chapter 64, conventionally called Mutual Blaming
    d. Chapter 58, conventionally called The Debate

6. Who are the two women specifically mentioned as the good examples in the Quran?
   a. Noah's wife and Mary
   b. Pharaoh's wife and Mary
   c. Lot's wife and Mary
   d. Moses' mother and Mary

7. "Say, 'Do you see that if it were from **God**, and you rejected it, and a witness from the Children of Israel testified to its similarity, and he has acknowledged, while you have turned arrogant? Surely, **God** does not guide the wicked people.'" With the fulfillment of the Quranic prophecy mentioned in chapter 74, the identity of the Jewish witness became evident. Who was that witness?
   a. Moses
   b. Saint Paul
   c. Ubayy b. Kab
   d. Rabbi Judah

8. Approximately how many books are there in the Torah?
   a. 20
   b. 40
   c. 60
   d. 70

9. Which messenger's name has been mentioned most frequently in the Quran?
   a. Abraham
   b. Adam
   c. Moses
   d. Muhammad

10. Which one of the following names or attributes mentioned in the Quran?
   a. Abu Lahab
   b. Yazeed
   c. Marwan b. Al Hakam
   d. Khuzaimah b. Al Ansary

11. How many times does the word "God" occur in the Quran?
    a. 2689
    b. 2888
    c. 2698
    d. 114

12. How many Chapters begin with letters (initials)?
    a. 19
    b. 29
    c. 38
    d. 39

13. In what form did angels visit the prophet Lot?
    a. Angel
    b. Human male
    c. Human female
    d. None of the above

14. Put the words separated by the slashes in the correct sequence to form a Quranic verse. Then which part is the third in the sequence? alone / your Lord / when you preach / using the Quran / they run in aversion
    a. using the Quran
    b. alone
    c. your Lord
    d. when you preach

15. Which one of these is NOT an attribute of God?
    a. The Steadfast (Al Sabbur)
    b. The Peace (Al Salam)
    c. The Most Trusted (Al Muman)
    d. The Designer (Al Musawir)

16. How many lunar years are equal 100 solar years?
    a. 101
    b. 103
    c. 109
    d. 97

17. "From among his descendants was Abraham. He came to his Lord with a pure heart. When he said to his father and his people: 'What are you serving? Is it fabricated gods, instead of God that you want? What do you say of the Lord of the worlds?' Then he looked towards the stars. He said, 'I am ill!'"   Why did Abraham look at the stars?
    a. His people were worshiping the stars
    b. At that time Abraham was worshiping the stars
    c. He expected a punishment from the sky
    d. All of the above

18. Knowing the fact that there are 114 chapters in the Quran, which one of these is a mathematical property?
    a. Total of the chapter numbers (1+2+3+ .... +114 = 6555) is divisible by 19
    b. Total of the 19 chapter numbers between the missing *Basmala* and extra *Basmala* (9+10+ .... +27=342), is divisible by 19
    c. If you multiply the number of initialed chapters with the number of chapters (29x114 = 3306) is divisible by 19
    d. All of the above

19. Based on the Quranic information about Abraham, which one of the following is true?
    a. He broke all the statues in his town and then challenged the idol worshipers.
    b. He wanted proof from God to believe in resurrection
    c. He never asked forgiveness for his polytheist father
    d. He never practiced idol-worship

20. The verse 2:142 answers critics regarding the change of the direction (*qibla*). But the divine command for change does not exist in the Quran. What do we learn from the absence of this command?
    a. There is no abrogation in the Quran. (No verse invalidated previous verse).
    b. Muhammad received some revelations beside Quran; but they were personal.
    c. God tests peacemakers in different points. In this case, conservative peacemakers who were trying to compromise with idol worshipers have been exposed and eliminated.
    d. All of the above.

Test 2

1. Fill in the space in the following verse: "Every community must receive a(n) ...."
   a. book
   b. retribution
   c. warner
   d. angel

2. Fill in the space in the following verse: "He said, 'my lord, give me a .... 'He said, 'your .... is that you will not speak to the people for three consecutive nights.'"
   a. miracle
   b. punishment
   c. responsibility
   d. sign

3. Fill in the space in the following verse: "God and His angels .... the prophet. O you who believe, you shall........ him, and regard him as he should be regarded."
   a. praise
   b. help and support
   c. reward
   d. send blessing on

4. How many men did Moses select from among his people to go to God's appointed audience?
   a. 40
   b. 60
   c. 70
   d. 19

5. Which chapter does NOT have the Basmala in the beginning?
   a. Chapter 9, conventionally called Ultimatum or Repentance
   b. Chapter 27, conventionally called The Ant
   c. Chapter 48, conventionally called The Victory
   d. Chapter 32, conventionally called Prostration

6. Which chapter has two Basmalas?
   a. Chapter 9, conventionally called Ultimatum or Repentance
   b. Chapter 27, conventionally called The Ant
   a. Chapter 40, conventionally called Forgiver
   b. Chapter 96, conventionally called The Embryo

7. "He escaped to the loaded ship. He rebelled, and joined the losers. The fish swallowed him, and he was the one to blame." Who was that person?
   a. Noah
   b. Pharaoh
   c. Zan-Noon
   d. None of them

8. Who argued with God on behalf of Lot's people?
   a. Lot
   b. Lot's wife
   c. Abraham
   d. None of them

9. The Quran gives us some important signs of the approaching end of the world. One of them is splitting the moon (See 54:1), which was fulfilled by splitting rocks from the moon. This important sign and the analysis of the Quran by computer coincided. What was the year of these two important events?
   a. 1969
   b. 1971
   c. 1974
   d. 1976

10. Who employed and controlled the jinns?
    a. David
    b. Solomon
    c. Jesus
    d. Muhammad

11. What does the number 118123 remind you of?
    a. Total of the letters in whole initialed chapters
    b. The total of verse numbers where the word Allah (God) occurs
    c. The total of all numbers mentioned in the Quran
    d. None of the above

12. How many times does "Q" occur in the two "Q" initialed chapters?
    a. 114
    b. 152
    c. 190
    d. 209

13. Which months are the sacred months?
    a. 12, 1, 2, 3 (Zul-Hijja, Muharram, Safar, Rabi 1)
    b. 7, 8, 9, 12 (Rajab, Shaban, Ramadan, Zul-Hijja)
    c. 7, 11, 12, 1 (Rajab, Zul-Qada, Zul-Hijja, Muharram)
    d. Only Ramadan

14. Quran sometimes uses the word "iblis" for Satan, which means "the confused". The word "insan" (human) perhaps is a derivative of NaSaYa, which means "the forgetful". What does "Jinn" mean?
    a. Fighter
    b. The one created from the fire
    c. Liar
    d. The one that is invisible to humans or the one that covers

15. Which one of the following is NOT an attitude of monotheists?
    a. Stern and uncompromising against ingrates
    b. Avoid vain talk
    c. Follow hadith and sunna besides the Quran
    d. Question the religious teachings of their parents and the majority around them

16. Which one of the following statements is wrong?
    a. All the stars, planets, plants and animals are submitters
    b. All the prophets were initially humiliated and have been oppressed
    c. Everybody will see Hell
    d. Every soul has to taste the death

17. In verse 20:17 God asks Moses about his staff, "What is this in your hand, Moses?" What could be one of the reasons for such a question?
    a. To teach him that it is not a staff
    b. To make him confess about the usage and importance of the staff
    c. To inform us
    d. All of the above

18. Which one of the following may NOT be used to support the fact that Muhammad was literate?
    a. Chronologically, the first revelation was "Read", and the second revelation was "The pen"
    b. The different spelling of some words and their role in the mathematical composition of the Quran
    c. A revelation and recording of a book lasting 23 years
    d. The manuscripts in museums known as Muhammad's letters to kings

19. "..He creates you in your mother's bellies, creation after creation, in three layers of darkness." What one of the following is the best understanding of the three layers of darkness?
    a. The dark periods of birth, inside the womb and grave
    b. The mother's belly which isolated from light, sound and smell that come from outside
    c. The three trimesters of development of a fetus
    d. To be unaware of time, space and matter

20. Which one of the following is wrong?
    a. Every submitter in peace (*muslim*) is an acknowledging person (*mumin*), but every acknowledging person is not a submitter in peace.
    b. The worst enemies of the acknowledging people come from among Jews and the *mushriks* (polytheists).
    c. An acknowledging person (*mumin*) is a Quranic term which has not been used for those who mix their conviction with *shirk*.
    d. People have been divided into three main categories in their relation with God: God-conscious, ingrates and hypocrites.

Test 3

1. Fill in the space in the following verse: ".......... had come to you before with proofs, but you remained in doubt regarding what he came to you with, until when he died, you said, 'God will not send any messenger after him.' It is such that God sends astray he who is a transgressor, doubter."
   a. Moses
   b. Solomon
   c. Joseph
   d. Jesus

2. Fill in the space in the verse below: "They took .... to be lords besides God, and the Messiah son of Mary, while they were only commanded to serve One god, there is no god but He, be He glorified for what they set up."
   a. their children
   b. statues
   c. money and career
   d. their religious leaders and scholars

3. Fill in the space in the verse below: "Those who rejected amongst the people of the book and those who set up partners would not leave until proof came to them."
   a. proof
   b. kingship
   c. victory
   d. promise

4. Which attributes of God has the greatest gematrical value?
   a. Wahid (One)
   b. Majid (Glorious)
   c. Zul Maarij (Possessor of the highest height)
   d. Zul Fadlil Azym (Possessor of infinite grace)

5. It has nineteen verses and it is the only chapter which ends with the word God, which is the nineteenth word God from the end of the Quran. Which chapter is that?
   a. Chapter 96
   b. Chapter 87
   c. Chapter 82
   d. Chapter 73

6. Which one of these commandments does not exist in the Quran?
   a. Read
   b. Grow beard
   c. Help others
   d. Use your mind

7. Used a novel technology to construct a barrier to protect oppressed people from two imperialist nations.
   a. The one with two generations
   b. David
   c. Gog and Magog
   d. Saul

8. Which list is in chronological order?
   a. Noah, Abraham, Joseph, Moses, David
   b. Abraham, Noah, Moses, David, Joseph
   c. Abraham, Noah, Joseph, David, Moses
   d. Noah, Abraham, David, Moses, Joseph

9. Which messenger had a speech problem?
   a. Zachariah
   b. Job
   c. Moses
   d. None of the messengers

10. He had 12 children, each becoming the leader of a Jewish tribe?
    a. Abraham
    b. Jacob
    c. Joseph
    d. None of the above

11. How many different numbers are mentioned in the Quran?
    a. 19
    b. 29
    c. 30
    d. 57

12. The word Month (*shahr*) is mentioned 12 times in the Quran. How many times does the word Day (*yawm*) occur in the Quran?
    a. 19
    b. 30
    c. 354
    d. 365

13. Who received the Torah (the Old Testament)
    a. Moses
    b. Moses and Aaron
    c. Prophets sent to the Children of Israel
    d. None of them

14. When Mary suffered from the pain of the birth pangs, what did God provide for her as a pain relief?
    a. ripe dates
    b. ripe dates and stream
    c. walking and talking
    d. not to talk with people

15. Verse 3:7 teaches us that the Quran consists of straightforward and multiple-meaning verses. Which one of the following is NOT a multiple meaning verse?
    a. And this is a revelation from the Lord of the universe. The Honest Spirit/Gabriel brought it down.
    b. "..And we sent down to you this message, to proclaim/explain for the people everything that is sent down to them."
    c. "When we abrogate any miracle/verse, or cause it to be forgotten, we bring a better miracle/verse or at least an equal one. Do you not know that God is Omnipotent?"
    d. "This is an honorable Quran. In a perfectly preserved book. None can grasp/touch it, except the righteous/clean one."

16. Which one of the following is wrong?
    a. Jihad was in the past and it is not valid at the present time and in the future.
    b. Fighting in the cause of God is always for self defense.
    c. If you are oppressed you can use bad language.
    d. Religious education is so important, even in the war time some people must stay behind for the education.

17. What was the number of the people of the cave?
    a. 5 plus their dog
    b. 6 plus their dog
    c. 7 plus their dog
    d. Only few people knows the correct number

18. There were four forces against Moses and his supporters: politics, economics, military, and religious leaders. What was the representative of these four forces respectively?
    a. Pharaoh, magicians, Haman, Qarun
    b. Pharaoh, Haman, Qarun, magicians
    c. Haman, Qarun, Pharaoh, magicians
    d. Pharaoh, Qarun, Haman, magicians

19. In which case did jealousy NOT play an important role?
    a. The first murder
    b. Throwing Joseph into the well
    c. Disbelief of Lot's wife
    d. Rejection of Jewish people of the messengership of Muhammad

20. Which of the following is not mentioned as a prophet?
    a. Saleh
    b. Aaron
    c. John
    d. Elisha

Test 4

1. Fill in the space in the following verse: "They remained in their cave for three hundred years, and increased ...."
    a. seven
    b. nine
    c. nineteen
    d. ten

2. Fill in the space in the following verse: "He made the earth .... "
    a. flat
    b. from water
    c. egg-shaped
    d. light

3. Fill in the space in the following verse: "They said, 'O ...., you were well liked amongst us before this. Do you deter us from serving what our fathers served? We are in serious doubt as to what you are inviting us.'"
    a. Moses
    b. Saleh
    c. Abraham
    d. Solomon

4. Which one of these Arabic terms in the Quran, when used in connection with humans, is/are usually carry a negative meaning?
    a. Hadith
    b. Sunna
    c. Ijma
    d. All of the above

5. Choose the one that delivered the message for a messenger:
    a. Ant
    b. Horse
    c. Hoopoe
    d. Clouds

6. There is a numerical connection between the gematrical value of "Adam" and one of the following. Which one?
   a. Eve
   b. Number of bones in human body
   c. Jesus
   d. Number of chromosomes in the human species

7. Which one of these messengers never was a polytheist?
   a. Saleh
   b. John
   c. Muhammad
   d. Rashad

8. Only one of the companions of the prophet Muhammad has been mentioned by name in the Quran, which one?
   a. Abu Bakr
   b. Omar
   c. Zayd
   d. Ali

9. Who claimed his messengership when he was a child in the crib?
   a. Jesus
   b. Moses
   c. Abraham
   d. Ishmael

10. What was the name of Medina, during the time of Muhammad?
   a. Medina
   b. Uhud
   c. Yathrib
   d. Badr

11. Some initials are followed by statements in the same verse, but some verses contain only initial letters. How many chapters have only initial letters in their first verses?
   a. 7
   b. 17
   c. 19
   d. 29

12. How many words are there in the first chapter of the Quran, conventionally known Al-Fateha (The Key)?
    a. 7
    b. 17
    c. 19
    d. 29

13. "O you who acknowledge, do not come near the contact prayer while you are drunk, until you know what you are saying..." Which one of the following is implied by this verse?
    a. Acknowledgers are allowed to use intoxicants while they are not praying.
    b. This verse has been abrogated by the verses prohibiting the intoxicants.
    c. If a believer is duped by Satan and is intoxicated he should not be allowed to enter masjids.
    d. None of the above.

14. "He is the One who merges the two bodies of water. This is fresh and palatable and this is salty and bitter. He made between them a partition and an inviolable barrier." What could be that barrier?
    a. Evaporation
    b. A block of water with different density
    c. Land
    d. Water surface tension

15. Which one of the statements below is correct?
    a. Quran was revealed to Muhammad gradually
    b. Every submitter (*muslim*) is not an acknowledger of truth (*mumin*)
    c. Only messengers and prophets receive revelation
    d. Muhammad was the last messenger

16. What is the psychological effect of bright yellow on people?
    a. Gives pleasure
    b. Makes nervous
    c. Relaxes the eyes
    d. None of the above

17. Which one of the following is correct?
    a. One can give the charity (*zaka*) to his wife
    b. Acknowledgers do not die
    c. Satan can not dupe a believer
    d. Satan was the first racist

18. Which one of the following is wrong?
    a. A divorced woman shall wait three menstruations before marrying another man.
    b. If an oath is violated by a submitter who can not afford feeding poor, he or she must fast three days as atonement for violating the oath.
    c. People will be stratified into three kinds after the resurrection.
    d. Divorce may be retracted three times

19. Which one is wrong?
    a. During the time of Muhammad the *mushriks* (polytheists) were not worshiping statues.
    b. *Mushriks* believe in God.
    c. We can not pray for forgiveness for the *musriks*.
    d. Muhammad was never a *mushrik*.

20. Which one of the following can NOT be an idol for people?
    a. God's messengers
    b. God's message
    c. Leaders
    d. Ego

Test 5

1. Fill in the space in the following verse: " We do not duplicate a ....., or make it forgotten, unless We bring one which is like it or even greater. Did you not know that **God** is capable of all things?"
    a. Revelation
    b. Miracle
    c. Verse
    d. Law

2. Fill in the space in the following verse: "They said, 'O Shuayb, does your .... order you that we leave what our fathers served, or that we do not do with our money as we please? You are the compassionate, the sane'!"
    a. Faith
    b. Religion
    c. Prayer (*sala*)
    d. Friends

3. Fill in the space in the following verse: "Do not uphold what you have no knowledge of. For the hearing, eyesight, and .... , all these are held responsible for that."
    a. hands
    b. tongue
    c. mind
    d. heart

4. Which chapter has the maximum repetition of the same verse (31 times)?
    a. Mary (19)
    b. S (Saad, 38)
    c. Luqman (31)
    d. Most Gracious (Rahman, 55)

5. Which one of the following lists the chapters in their conventional names, according to their order in the Quran?
   a. Hood, Joseph, Thunder, Abraham, Al-Hijr, The Bee
   b. Joseph, Hood, Thunder, Abraham, The Bee, Al-Hijr
   c. Hood, Joseph, Thunder, Abraham, Al-Hijr, The Bee
   d. Hood, Joseph, Al-Hijr, Thunder, Abraham, The Bee

6. Which verse decrees the correct "*shahada*" (testimony), known as the first pillar of Islam?
   a. 3:18
   b. 3:81
   c. 6:19
   d. 63:1

7. How many chapters have been named with the name of God?
   a. 3
   b. 4
   c. 5
   d. 6

8. Who was the messenger to Madyan?
   a. Shuayb
   b. Hood
   c. Saleh
   d. Job

9. Which incident did the acknowledgers accept as the beginning of their calendar after Prophet Muhammad?
   a. The revelation of the Quran
   b. Immigration from Mecca to Medina
   c. The birth of Muhammad
   d. The death of Muhammad

10. He was appointed as a king (commander) for Moses' people on their request. Under his command they defeated a large army by God's leave. Who was that commander?
   a. Saul
   b. Goliath
   c. Samarian
   d. None of them

11. What was the age of Noah when he died?
    a. 90
    b. 760
    c. 950
    d. 1000

12. How many un-initialed chapters are there between the first initialed chapter (chapter 2) and the last initialed chapter (chapter 68)?
    a. 19
    b. 29
    c. 39
    d. None of them

13. Which one of the following is mentioned as a proper noun in the Quran?
    a. Ahmad
    b. Eva
    c. Rashad
    d. None of them

14. Quran gives us some examples to prove resurrection. Which one of the following cannot be an example for resurrection?
    a. Blooming of flowers in the spring
    b. Waking up of sleep
    c. Burning wood
    d. Blowing air into a balloon

15. Cain, son of Adam, killed his brother. "So God sent forth a raven to scratch the land and show him how to bury his brother's body." What do we learn from the verse above?
    a. Despite his arrogance human being needs to learn many things from animals.
    b. Ravens bury their species' corpses.
    c. We should not cremate the corpses.
    d. The first two, i.e., (a) and (b).

16. "We have given you seven of the pairs and the great Quran." What is the traditional interpretation of the "seven pairs"?
    a. The chapter Key (*Al-Fateha*), which its seven verses are repeated in the prayers
    b. The seven longest chapters
    c. The seven H.M. initialed chapters or seven miracles
    d. All of the above

17. "We have given you seven of the pairs and the great Quran." The seven pairs can not be interpreted as the chapter Key. Which one of the following can not support this claim?
    a. The word "Quran" is mentioned after the seven pairs
    b. The word "given" is used instead of "sent"
    c. The verses before and after this verse are about the end of the world and Muhammad's period
    d. The chapter "The Key" was revealed after this verse

18. Which one of these insects and animals are not mentioned in the Quran?
    a. spider
    b. lion
    c. lizard/gecko
    d. crow

19. Which one of the following is a Quranic statement?
    a. You should divide yourselves into sects
    b. The Quran alone cannot guide you to salvation.
    c. Muhammad was the highest of all messengers.
    d. None of the above.

20. "A1L30M40; The Romans have won, at the lowest point on the earth. But after their victory, they will be defeated. In a few more years. The decision before and after is for God, and on that day those who acknowledge will rejoice. With God's victory. God gives victory to whom He wishes; He is the Noble, the Compassionate." Muslims sided with those (Persians) who fought against Romans. Which one of the following, if true, supports our preferred reading?

    a. The verb "*GHaLaBa*" can be read differently than the traditional translations. Instead of reading the verb in 30:2 as "*ghulibat*" (were defeated) it could be read as "*ghalabat*" which means just the opposite, "defeated."

    b. The prophecy of the verse was realized in 636 four years after the death of Muhammad, when Muslims confronted the army of Byzantine Empire around Yarmuk river, in one of the most significant battles in history.

    c. The six-day war, Yarmuk, occurred in area near the Sea of Galilee and Dead Sea, which are located in the lowest land depression on earth, 200-400 meters below sea level.

    d. All of the above.

Test 6
(Not Classified)

1. Fill the blank in the following verse: "The men are to support the women by what God has gifted them over one another and for what they spend of their money. The reformed women are devotees and protectors of privacy what God has protected. As for those women from whom you fear disloyalty, then you shall advise them, abandon them in the bedchamber,..............................; if they obey you, then do not seek a way over them; God is High, Great."
    a. and separate from them
    b. beat them
    c. scare them
    d. divorce them

2. Fill the blank in the following verse: "Fight those who do not acknowledge God nor the Last day from among the people who received the book; they do not forbid what God and His messenger have forbidden, and they do not uphold the system of truth; until they pay the ...., in humility." (9:29)
    a. Reparation
    b. Tax
    c. Price
    d. Poor

3. "If he divorces you, his Lord will substitute other wives in your place who are better than you; peacefully surrendering (to God), acknowledging, devout, repentant, serving,
    ...." (66:5)

    a. Fasters, widows, and virgins
    b. Active in their societies, responsive, and foremost ones.
    c. Fasters, happy, and virgins
    d. Quiet, giving, and committed

4. Fill the blank in the following verse: "Say: 'O people, I am God's messenger to you all. The One who has the sovereignty of heavens and earth, there is no god but He; He gives life and causes death.' So acknowledge God and His .... (*ummi*), who acknowledges God and His words; and follow him that you may be guided." (7:158)
   a. Illiterate
   b. Innumerate
   c. Gentle
   d. **Gentile**

5. Which one of these is not a Quranic description of Muhammad?
   a. Role model
   b. Mercy for the people
   c. Last messenger
   d. A human like you

6. Why the word *aya* should be translated a sign/miracle rather than revelation in verse 2:106, below: "We do not duplicate (or abrogate) any sign (*aya*) or cause it to be forgotten, unless we produce a better, or at least an equal one. Do you not know that God is Omnipotent?"
   a. The singular form *aya*, in all its 84 occurrences in the Quran is always used to mean sign or miracle.
   b. There should be no contradiction among verse of the Quran (4:82), so there should be no abrogation in the Quran.
   c. The Quran does not mark verses as abrogated and there are sectarian differences on which verse is abrogator (*nasih*) and which is abrogated (*mansuh*).
   d. All of the above.

7. Why the story about Muhammad's illiteracy is a fabrication?
   a. The word *ummy* does not mean illiterate, but gentile
   b. Muhammad was smart enough to learn the 28 letters in Arabic alphabet.
   c. There are some homophone words in the Arabic Quran (For instance, compare the Bism of Basmala and verse 96:1).
   d. All of the above

8. The Quran mentions communities as well as individuals who received retribution because of their transgressions. Which one of these people were punished primarily because of their corrupt business activities:
   a. People of Noah
   b. People of Thamud
   c. People of Madyan or Woods
   d. People of Aad

9. Historical and archeological evidence shows during the revelation of the Quran Arabs were using their alphabet also as a numerical system, like their counterparts Jews and Romans. What is that numerical system is called?
   a. Alif-Ba-Ta
   b. Abjad
   c. Huruf
   d. All of the above

10. Which animal is not mentioned in the Quran?
   a. Bear
   b. Monkey
   c. Horse
   d. Sheep

11. Which insect is not mentioned in the Quran?
   a. Mosquito
   b. Ant
   c. Bee
   d. Flee

12. How many verses of the Quran contain all the 14 letters which are used in initials?
   a. 19
   b. 38
   c. 114
   d. 266

13. Which one of these descriptions of Hell shows that the description is allegorical?
    a. There sulfur and acid is served
    b. Its fire burns the skins
    c. Inside its fire there is a bitter tree
    d. All of the above

14. According to the Quran the idea of being saved in the Day of Judgment through intercession (*shafaa*), is a polytheistic lie (see verse 4:48). The only testimony that is allowed in the Day of Judgment is testimony for truth. The Quran informs us about only one statement, which will be uttered by Muhammad in the Day of Judgment. What is that statement?
    a. My Lord, my people have deserted my sunna
    b. My Lord, my people have deserted this Quran and my hadith and sunna
    c. My Lord, my people have deserted this Quran and my family
    d. My Lord, my people have deserted this Quran

15. The Quran lists important characteristics of a leader. What are they?
    a. Knowledge and health
    b. Wealth and health
    c. Being from Muhammad's lineage and knowledge
    d. All of the above

16. Which one of these statements on nature is not found in the Quran?
    a. The earth and havens were a single mass and they were separated from each other and are continuously expanded
    b. The earth is round, resembling an egg
    c. God did not use evolution in the creation
    d. Everything is created in pairs

17. The Quran repeatedly reminds us of sharing our blessings, including wealth, with those who are less fortunate. Which one of these is not listed among the group recommended for the reception of charity?
    a. Family and the relatives
    b. Orphans and the needy
    c. The wayfarer
    d. Clergymen

18. Which one of these is prohibited by the Quran?
    a. Drawing an imaginary picture of Muhammad
    b. Praying nude in one's privacy
    c. Playing guitar
    d. None of the above

19. Which one of these are accurate rendering of 74:29?
    a. **Yusuf Ali**:   "darkening and changing the color of man"
    b. **Pickthall**:   "It shrivelleth the man"
    c. **Irving**:   "as it shrivels human (flesh)"
    d. **Shakir**:   "It scorches the mortal"
    e. **M. Ali**:   "It scorches the mortal"
    f. **Dawood**:   "it burns the skins of men"
    g. **M. Asad**:   "making (all truth) visible to mortal man"
    h. **R. Khalifa**: "obvious to all the people"
    i. **Reformist**:   "obvious to humankind"

20. Verse 12:68 informs us about an interesting tactic by Jacob, "When
    they entered from where their father had commanded them, it would
    not have availed them in the least against **God**, but it was out of a
    concern in Jacob's person. Since We have taught him, he had certain
    knowledge; but most people do not know?" Using your
    understanding of the Quran, which of the following understanding is
    more in congruent with the Quran?
    a. To protect his children from "bad eye." Some people have
        bad eyes; when they envy a person and look at them with
        their eyes, they may cause problems for them.
    b. Jacob put his sons in competition so that they would arrive in
        Egypt as soon as possible.
    c. Perhaps, Jacob thought that a crowded group on the
        Egyptian border would pull the attention of officers or spies,
        who might have been alert against immigration because of
        severe draught.
    d. None of the above

ANSWERS

Test 1

1.d See 38:35. Jonah and Jesus were not tested with wealth. Qarun failed, while Solomon recognized his weakness and repented for his indulgence.

2.a See 4:48; 4:153; 6:22-23. Many of those who associate partners with God in his powers, such as His creative, legislative, guiding, or judiciary powers, do not accept that they are indeed polytheists who associate partners with God.

3.c See verse 35:28.

4.b See chapter 40 for the claim of those who wish to limit God's plan to send messengers to every nation.

5.d Chapter 58 has the word God (Allah) in all its 22 verses.

6.b See verse 66:11

7.d See verse 46:10. In the 1980's, we learned that Rabi Juda, a French Jewish scholar who lived in eleventh century, had discovered a mathematical system based on the number 19, in the original parts of the Old Testament. The similarity and clarity of the discovery is impressive and fulfills the prophecy of this verse. Rabi Judah's discovery of 19 in the original parts of the Old Testament, and his correction of the modern text by using the code, together with a list of examples, was unveiled in an article authored by Joseph Dan and was published by the University of California in 1978 under the title *"Studies in Jewish Mysticism."* According to Dan's article, Rabi Juda claimed to have written 8 volumes on the code 19-based mathematical structure in the Hebrew Old Testament. Hopefully, one day some scholars will search and discover that important work.

8.b The Catholic version has a few more books. But, you know that this question does not measure directly one's knowledge of the Quran.

9.c Moses' name is mentioned 136 times in the Quran. Abraham 69 times, Adam and Jesus each 25 times, and Muhammad 4 times.

10.a See verse 111:1. The expression *Abu Lahab* means the "father of flame" or provocateur. Traditional commentaries tie this description to Muhammad's uncle Abd al-Uzza bin Ab al-Muttalib. Even if the first person who was implied by this verse were Muhammad's uncle, the chapter by using a metaphor rather than a proper name, refers to all despots and their allies who oppress people because of their ideas and convictions. In this chapter, the wife has two different roles: either she is supplying more fuel for her husband in support of his bigoted campaign against muslims, or she is supplying fuel for her husband who is burning himself with flames of hatred.

11.c   The word God (Allah) is mentioned in the numbered verses of the Quran exactly 2698 (19x142) times, excluding 9:129.

12.b   Twenty nine chapters of the Quran starts with letter/number combinations. For instance, chapter 2 starts with A1L30M40. The meaning of 14 different combinations of alphabet letters/numbers initializing 29 chapters of the Quran remained a secret for centuries until 1974. Many scholars attempted to understand the meaning of these initial letters with no results. A computerized study that started in 1969 revealed in 1974 a 19-based mathematical design that was prophesied in Chapter 74. The frequency of the 14 alphabet letters in 14 different combinations that initialize 29 chapters are an integral part of this mathematical structure. The number of chapters that starts with various letters/number combinations are: 2, 3, 7, 10, 11, 12, 13, 14, 15, 19, 20, 26, 27, 28, 29, 30, 31, 32, 36, 38, 40, 41, 42, 43, 44, 45, 46, 50, and 68.

13.b   See verse 29:31-33. "When Our messengers came to Abraham with good news, they then said, 'We are to destroy the people of such a town, for its people have been wicked.' He said, 'But Lot is in it!' They said, 'We are fully aware of who is in it. We will save him and his family, except his wife; she is of those doomed.' Thus when Our messengers came to Lot, they were mistreated, and he was embarrassed towards them. They said, 'Do not fear, and do not be saddened. We will save you and your family, except for your wife; she is of those doomed.' "

14.a   See verse 17:46. "We place shields over their hearts, that they should not understand it, and a deafness in their ears. When you mention your Lord in the Quran alone, they run away turning their backs in aversion."

Those who do not acknowledge the hereafter with certainty will not understand the Quran, and they will claim that the Quran is difficult or even impossible to understand on its own. See 54:17,22,32,40.

Traditional translations and commentaries somehow separate the word "Quran" from the adjective (*wahdahu* = alone, only) that follows it. They translate it as "Lord alone in the Quran." Though there are many verses emphasizing God's oneness (see 39:45), this verse could be understood as another one emphasizing that message. However, this could be only a secondary meaning of this particular verse, since the adjective *wahdehu* is used not after the word *Rab* (Lord) but after the word Quran. In Arabic if one wants to say 'Quran alone,' the only way of saying it is "*Quranun wahdahu.*" The mathematical structure of the Quran too confirms our translation. For instance, the word *wahdahu* is used for God in 7:70; 39:45; 40:12,84 and 60:4. If we add these numbers we get 361, or 19x19. However, if we add 17:46, where the word *wahdahu* is used for the Quran, the total is not in harmony with the great mathematical system.

15.a   Al-Sabbur (The Steadfast) is not an attribute of God. The Quran uses more than a hundred attributes for God, and attributes indicate continuity. Not every verb used for God can be considered an attribute. For instance, not every person who writes can be called a "writer." Furthermore, God's attributes are not necessarily Arabic. God sent messengers in many different languages to each nation, and informed them about His attributes in their languages. Thus, the Quran teaches us that to God belong all beautiful attributes. However, *hadith* books lists 99 attributes of which some cannot be considered "beautiful." The list, which is very popular among Sunni and Shiite mushriks and many people memorize, include "bad" names such as *al-Dar* (the one who harms). Quran tells us otherwise (42:30).

Those who have confused Arab nationalism with islam might criticize our use of the English word God in the English text, rather than the word Allah. We would like to pull the attention of those who are not intoxicated with *hadith* and *sunna* that promotes Arab culture to the following points: the word Allah is not a proper name; it is an Arabic word contraction of the article *Al* (the) and *Elah* (god). Also, see 2:165; 3:26; 6:12; 17:110; 20:52; 42:11; 58:7.

The Quran informs us that God has been sending messengers to every nation in their own language (14:4). In each language, names or attributes represented by different sounds and symbols are used for the creator. For instance, the Old Testament uses *Yehovah* or *Elohim*. The New Testament quotes from Jesus addressing to God as *Eloi* (my lord), which is very close to the Arabic word *Elahi* (my lord) (Mark 15:34).

Through distortion and mistranslations, some Biblical verses depict God as less than a perfect being. For instance, Judges 1:19 (powerless); Genesis 6:6-7 (fallible); Psalms 13:1; Lamentations 5:20 (forgetful); Genesis 3:8-10 (can't see); 1 Samuel 15:2-3 (cruel). For more on divine attributes in the Quran and the Bible, see 59:22-24.

The Quran contains more than a hundred attributes for God and they are designed letter by letter in accordance with the mathematical structure based on code 19. The studies of Prof. Adib Majul, which was continued by Edip Yuksel on the attributes of God, demonstrate an interlocking system. For instance, among the attributes of God, the frequency of only four of them are multiples of 19. They are *Shahyd* (Witness) 19, *Allah* (God) 2698, *Rahman* (Gracious) 57, *Rahym* (Compassionate) 114 times. When we analyze the attributes of God in according to their numerical values, we learn that only four of them are multiples of 19 and each correspond to the frequency of the other four: Wahid (One) 19, *Zulfadl-il Azym* (The Possessor of Great Bounty) 2698, *Majyd* (Glorious) 57, and *Jami* (Editor) 114. The details of this extraordinary and intricate mathematical design will be discussed in a book, which might be titled "On it 19" or "Nineteen: God's Signature in Nature and Scripture." See: 74:30.

16.b   There are 103 lunar years in a solar year. (See verse 18:25)

17.a   See verse 37:083-89. Abraham's people were worshiping stars and idols. (6:76-78)

18.d   None of them is significant in terms of numerical structure of the Quran.

19.d   See verses 21:51-70. A is wrong since Abraham left the biggest statue intact to make his point. B is wrong since Abraham wanted the sign for reassurance. C is wrong since he did ask forgiveness for his polytheist father. D is right since he never was a mushrik.

20.d   *Qibla* is a point to which we are supposed to turn while observing our daily prayers. *Kaba* played an important role in the Arabian Peninsula, and besides its historic importance, it provided economic and political benefits to the Arabs. *Kaba* is not a *holy* temple or shrine, but an annual gathering place for monotheists to commemorate God, to remember the struggles of monotheists throughout history, to get to know each other, to exchange information, to promote charity, to remember their commonalities regardless of their differences in color, culture and language, to discuss their political and economical issues amicably, and to improve their trade.

The Quran informs us that those who associate other authorities with God continued the tradition of Abraham, only in form. Before the verses ordering muslims to turn to *Kaba* as *qibla* were revealed, muslims, like mushriks were turning towards *Kaba*. Muslims suffering from the repression, oppression and torture of Meccan polytheists finally decided to emigrate to Medina and there they established a city-state. However, the Meccan theocratic oligarchy did not leave them alone. They organized several major war campaigns. The aggression of the Meccan oligarchy and the improving economic, politic and social relations between muslims and the people of the book, that is Christians and Jews, led muslims to turn to another uniting point. They picked Jerusalem. Nevertheless, God wanted muslims to turn back to their original *qibla*, *al-Masjid al-Haram* (the restricted place of prostration). We understand this from verses 2:142-145. These verses asking muslims to turn back to their former *qibla* in Mecca created a difficult test for some muslims living in Medina.

Those who preferred the advantages of personal, social and economic relations with the Christian and Jewish community in Medina and those who could not get over their emotional grievances against the Meccan community could not accept this change and reverted back from islam (2:142-144).

In brief, the verses ordering the change of *qibla* did not abrogate another verse, since there is not a single verse ordering muslims to turn to another *qibla*. If there is an abrogation, the decision of Muhammad and his companions to turn away from *Kaba* was abrogated.

Test 2

1.c   See 35:24

2.d   See 3:41

3.b   See 33:56. This verse is one of the most distorted and abused verses. We translated the word *salli ala* as "support/encourage." The same word occurs at 33:43 and 9:99,133. When these verses are studied comparatively, the traditional abuse and distortion becomes evident. Through this distortion, Muslim masses are led to commemorate and praise Muhammad's name day and night, rather than his Lord's and Master's name (33:41-42). Also, see 2:157.

4.c   See 7:155.

5.a   The reason why chapter 9 does not contain Basmala was questioned for centuries, and the conclusive answer came with the discovery of the code 19, prophesized in chapter 74. See 74:1-56; 1:1; 2:1; 13:38; 27:82; 38:1-8; 40:28-38; 46:10; 72:28.

6.b   See 27:30. The Basmala in this verse, compensates the missing Basmala from the beginning of chapter 9, exactly 19 chapters before. This extra Basmala here, thus, completes the number of Basmalas being 114 (19x6). See 1:1; 74:1-56

7.c   See 21:87. Yunus' (Jonah) name occurs in the Quran four times as Jonah. However, in the chapter that starts with the letter N or number 50, Jonah is referred to by the expression *Sahib ul-Hut*, that is, The Companion of the Fish (68:48). Referring to a messenger who has the letter N in his name, with an expression that does not contain the letter N, in a chapter where the letter N is counted (133 = 19 x 7), is a part of the Quran's mathematical system. Indeed, a unique expression in verse 21:87 supports this implied message

8.c   See 11:74.

9.a   See 54:1 and 74:1. *Hadith* narrators and collectors misunderstood this verse and tried to support their misunderstanding by the fabrication of a *hadith* reporting that Muhammad split the Moon by pointing at it with his finger. Some narrators did not stop there and claimed that half of the Moon fell in the backyard of Ali, Muhammad's son-in-law. The believers of this *hadith* are silent to the critical questions about the event. Why didn't populations of other countries witness this incredible event? If there were such an astronomical event, many people from China to Africa would have noticed and recorded it. Besides, this traditional interpretation contradicts the Quran, which specifically limits the signs given to Muhammad to be the signs contained in the

Quran alone (29:50-51). The splitting of the Moon was fulfilled when Apollo 11 landed on the Moon and astronauts took some rocks from the Moon back to earth in July 1969. The word *shaqqa*, which we translated as "split," does not necessarily mean splitting in half (see 80:26; 50:44). When this event was happening, Dr. Rashad Khalifa was uploading the Quran to his computer in St. Louis. Splitting the surface of the Moon was the start of his work, which led to the historical discovery of the miraculous mathematical system based on code 19, prophesied in chapter 74, which happened in 1974. Thus, the following verse relates to this discovery. See 74:1-56; 27:82; 38:1-8; 40:28-38; 46:10; 72:28.

10.b   See 21:82

11.b   When we add up the verse numbers of 85 chapters that contain the word Allah (God) we get 118123.

12.a   The frequency of "Q" in chapter 50 is 57, or 19x3. The letter "Q" occurs in the other Q-initialed chapter, i.e., chapter 42, exactly the same number of times, 57. The total occurrence of the letter "Q" in the two Q-initialed chapters is 114, which equals the number of chapters in the Quran. There are a few more details: The description of the Quran as "*Majid*" (Glorious) is correlated with the frequency of occurrence of the letter "Q" in each of the Q-initialed chapters. The word "*Majid*" has a gematrical value of 57. Chapter 42 consists of 53 verses, and 42+53 is 95, or 19x5. Chapter 50 consists of 45 verses, and 50+45 is 95, or 19x5.

13.a   Today's Sunni and Shiite mushriks consider *Rajab*, *Zul-Qada*, *Zul-Hijja*, and *Muharram* to be the Restricted Months (the 7th, 11th, 12th, and 1st months of lunar calendar). However, when we study 2:197,217; 9:2,5,36 and the names of known months, we will discover that real Restricted Months must be four consecutive months and they are *Zul-Hijja, Muharram, Safar, Rabi ul-Awal* (12th, 1st, 2nd, and 3rd months). The very name of the 12th month, *Zul-Hijja* (Contains *Haj*), gives us a clue that it is the first month of *haj* pilgrimage. When we start from the 12th month, the last of the Restricted Months becomes the 3rd month, *Rabi ul-Awal* (First Fourth), and the very name of this month also is revealing; it suggests that it is the fourth month of the Restricted Months. Then, why the qualification "First"? Well, the name of the following month provides an explanation: *Rabi ul-Akhir* (Second Fourth), which is the fourth month from the beginning of the year. In other words we have two months called "Fourth," the first one referring to the fourth restricted moth, with the second fourth referring to the fourth month of the lunar year. The word *rabi* (fourth) is used for seasons because each season is one fourth of a year. It is interesting that many of the crimes and distortions mentioned in the Quran have been committed by those who have abandoned the Quran for the sake of *hadith* and *sunna*; they repeated the same blunder of their polytheist ancestors.

14.d   Jinns are descendants of Satan (7:27), invisible (6:86; 72:1), made of energy (10:27), swift (27:10, 39), righteous and evildoers (72:11), possess power/ability to exit the atmosphere of Earth (72:8), and have physical powers not common to humans (27:39).

15.c   Here are some characteristics of those who acknowledge. They:

- Do not accept information on faith; critically evaluate it with their reason and senses (17:36)
- Ask the experts if they do not know (16:43)
- Use intelligence, reason and historical precedents to understand and carry out God's commands (7:179; 8:22; 10:100; 12:111; 3:137)
- Do not dogmatically follow the status-quo and tradition; are open to new ideas (22:1; 26:5; 38:7)
- Are open-minded and promote freedom of expression; listen to all views and follow the best (39:18)
- Do not follow conjecture (10:36,66; 53:28)
- Study God's creation in the heavens and land; explore the beginning of creation (2:164; 3:190; 29:20)
- Attain knowledge, since it is the most valuable thing in their appreciation of God (3:18; 13:13; 29:43,49)
- Are free individuals, do not follow crowds, and are not afraid of crowds (2:112; 5:54,69; 10:62; 39:36; 46:13)
- Do not follow the religion of your parents or your nation blindly (6:116; 12:103,112)
- Do not make profit from sharing God's Message with others (6:90; 36:21; 26:109-180)
- Read in order to know, and they read critically (96:1-5; 55:1-4)
- Do not ignore divine revelation and signs (25:73)
- Do not miss the main point by indulging in small and inconsequential details (2:67-71; 5:101-102; 22:67)
- Hold their judgment if they do not have sufficient information; do not rush into siding with a position (20:114)
- ...
- Speak the truth; do not lie, although stratagem is allowed against adversaries (8:7-8; 25:72; 33:70; 12:70-81)
- Are kind and forgiving (42:40,43)
- Are active, dynamic, creative and courageous people (2:30-34; 4:75-77; 15:28-30)
- Are not egoistic and proud (25:43; 17:37)
- Are steadfast and humble (31:17-18)

- Are brave (33:23)
- Do not lose hope; are optimistic (12:87; 39:53)
- Walk humbly on earth and when harassed by ignorant people; they ignore the harassers with dignity and respond them by saying "peace" (25:72: 29:63)
- Hold firmly to principles, but are flexible in methods (2:67-71, 142; 3:103; 5:54; 22:67)
- Are not proud of their accomplishments, and are not saddened by their losses (57:23)
- Seek unity not division; do not divide themselves due to jealousy (3:103; 6:159; 61:4; 42:14)
- Put moral considerations uppermost, but do not disregard their due material interests (28:77)
- Fulfill promises (17:34)
- Eat and drink moderately, and avoid intoxicants and gambling (7:31; 2:219)
- Dress decently (24:30-31)
- Do not ridicule or mock one another (49:11)
- Abstain from vain talk (23:4)
- Do not discriminate based on gender and race; they know that superiority is only through God-consciousness (49:13)
- Are loyal to what they have been entrusted and keep their pledges (23:9)
- Treat everyone with civility and give greetings to all (2:83; 28:55; 43:89; 4:86)
- Do not escape from problems, but rather actively focus on problems to solve them equitably, even if the solution requires a fight (49:9)
- Avoid suspicion, spying and backbiting among the monotheists; seek peace, since they are only brothers and sisters (49:9-10,12)
- Do not follow monarchs, princes, emirs, sultans, except when they are forced; obey those who are in charge among themselves, and when they dispute in any matter they refer it to God and the messenger (4:59)
- Are the party of God (58:22)
- Do not aggress, but defend themselves against aggression (7:33; 42:39)
- ...
- Serve God alone and do not associate partners in His authority (17:22-23)
- Dedicate themselves to God alone; they do not kill unjustly, and do not commit adultery (29:68)

- Believe in God and live righteously (2:62, 112)
- Love God, the Truth, more than anything else (5:54; 9:23)
- Do not fear mankind, but fear God (5:44; 33:37, 39)
- Maintain the contact prayers with God (23:10)
- Repent for their sins (29:70)
- …
- Respect and honor their parents (17:23-24)
- Love their spouses and treat them with care and compassion (30:21)
- Give charities to relatives, the poor and destitute and towards public welfare (9:60; 17:26)
- …
- Practice consultations to solve social and political problems (42:36)
- Act justly, do not commit evil and rule according to God's laws, i.e. justice, truth and mercy (4:58, 135; 5:8; 7:28-29; 5:44)
- Do not turn their cheeks arrogantly from people, nor roam the earth insolently, since they know that God does not like the arrogant show offs (31:18; 57:23)
- Perform prayers and other rites of worship, without quarrelling over methodology, and they share their blessings with those who have less than they have (98:5; 22:67)
- Obey just leaders, respect, honor and support them, but they do not idolize them (4:59; 33:56; 9:30-31)
- Do not practice bribery and corruption (2:188)
- Do not practice usury, but they practice charity (2:275-80)
- Give charity in moderation (29:67)
- Are honest and fair in financial and economic dealings (6:152)
- Do not bear false witness (29:71)
- Are not extravagant and wasteful, nor are they stingy (17:26-29)
- Save lives and do not kill except in the cause of justice (17:33)
- Respond equally, but they know that forgiveness is the best route (2:179; 13:14; 45:14; 64:14)
- Do not devour the properties of orphans (17:34)
- Enter into marriage with believers, do not marry disbelievers, and they do not commit adultery (5:5; 23:6-7; 30:21; 17:32)
- …
- Are not apathetic (5:79)
- Enjoin good and forbid evil (3:104)
- Hasten to do righteous work (3:114)
- Are active towards betterment (23:5)
- Support each other in the cause of God (8:74)

- Raise knowledgeable people in the society in order to learn the laws (9:122)
- Cooperate and help each other in good works; do not cooperate in evil works (5:2)
- Fight in the cause of justice and truth with their wealth and their lives (4:75; 9:111)
- Promote legal education (9:122)
- Persevere in any good effort and do not fear to face difficulties and hardships; success comes only after hardships (2:45, 177; 94:5-8)
- Fight for the rights of those who are oppressed (4:75)
- Seek peace (2:208; 4:90; 8:61; 2:208)
- Are progressive (15:24; 74:37)
- Reform themselves and are reformers (6:48,54; 7:35,56,142; 11:117; 12:101; 21:72,105)

(Thanks to Kassim Ahmad of Malaysia for his contribution in the compilation of this list.)

16.b   For A, see 41:11; for C, see ; and for D see 3:185.

17.d   Surely, God knew what was in Moses' hand. The following verses show that the question was a rhetorical one. See the Old Testament, Exodus 4:1-9.

18.d   Those letters could be forgery or written by others upon Muhammad's dictation.

19.c   See 39:6. Option A is vague and it does not add up to three. Option B is arbitrary since it excludes other sensory information without justification, such as taste and tactile perception. D is also arbitrary since it excludes energy, order, natural laws, etc.

20.a   Option A contradicts 49:14. Option B is supported by 5:82 "You will find the people with greatest animosity towards those who acknowledge are the Jews and those who set up partners; and you will find the closest in affection to those who acknowledge are those who said, 'We are Nazarenes;' that is because amongst them are Priests and Monks, and they are not arrogant." For option C, see 6:82; and for option D see 2:1-20.

Test 3

1.c   See 40:34. Similarly, Jews rejected John the Baptist and Jesus, and Christians rejected Muhammad.

2.d   See 9:31

3.a   See 98:1

4.d   The gematrical or numerical value of *WaHeD* is 19, *MaJYD* 57, *ZuL M'AaReJ* 1051, and of *Zul FaDL AL-'AZYM* is 2698, which is numerically the greatest of all attributes.

5.c

6.b

7.a   See 18:83-99

8.a

9.c   See 20:27

10.b   Jacob or Israel is the father of Jews. For the story of his twelve sons, see chapter 12.

11.c   The Quran mentions 30 different cardinal numbers: 1, 2, 3, 4, 5, 6, 7, 8, 9, 10, 11, 12, 19, 20, 30, 40, 50, 60, 70, 80, 99, 100, 200, 300, 1000, 2000, 3000, 5000, 50000, & 100000. The sum of these numbers is 162146, which equals 19x8534. And 30 is the 19th composite number.

12.d   The frequency of the word *YaWM* (day) in its singular form in the Quran is exactly 365 times, thereby creating a nusemantic relationship between the word DAY and SOLAR YEAR rather than DAY and LUNAR YEAR, thus rejecting the claim of those who wish impose the knowledge of medieval Arabic culture, complete with the use of a lunar year, onto the Quran. However, the plural word of day *aYyAM* (days) occurring 27 times and the dual form *YaWMayn* (two days) occurring 3 times, relate to the approximate number of days both in a lunar and solar month. Similar nusemantic relationships are extensive and were first observed by an Egyptian scholar Abdurazzaq al-Nawfal in the 1960's and was published in Al-ijaz ul-Adady fil-Quran il-Karym (The Numeric Miracle/Challenge in the Quran). For the prophecy regarding the mathematical structure of the Quran, see 74:30.

13.c   The Torah is known as the name of the book given to Moses. However, this common knowledge might be wrong. The Quran nowhere mentions that the Torah was given to Moses. The word Torah occurs 18 times in the Quran and it refers to the collection of books given to Jewish prophets excluding the *Injeel* delivered by Jesus. Though the name of the book(s) given to Moses is not mentioned, it is described with various adjectives such as *Furqan* (the distinguisher), *Emam* (the

48

leader), *Rahma* (mercy), *Noor* (light) and *Huda* (guidance). There is ample scholarly work indicating that current books of the Old Testament were extensively tampered with and written by Ezra and other rabbis. See 2:59; 2:79; 9:30-31. Also, see the Old Testament, Jeremiah 8:8.

14.b   See 19:23-25. The recommendation to Mary has medical benefits. The sound of water and mature dates have a regulating effect on human muscles and thus reduce the birth pain. Indeed, some modern birth clinics provide birth-in-water services. The oxytocin found in dates regulates contraction and stimulates lactation, and thus is given to pregnant women as a drug to ease their labor. This verse also gives a clue regarding the season in which Jesus was born. In the Middle East, dates get ripe in the end of September, and in the beginning of October.

15.a   Honest Spirit or Gabriel refers to the same entity or concept.

16.a   Option B is supported by 9:5,29; 8:19; 47:35; 60:7-9. Option C is supported by 4:148; Option D is supported by 9:122.

17.d   Since verse 18:22 states that only few people would not know their accurate number, thus the popularly accepted number 7 cannot be the correct one. Verses 18:9-27 use a very curious language. These 19 verses contain numerous key words that strongly imply that the story of the cave have double meaning like the verses in chapter 74, and the second meaning is about a prophecy of a mathematical miracle. I have already observed examples of a hidden mathematical design and God the most Wise will unveil it when the right time comes. When the secrets contained in the cave is revealed by divine permission, it will prove once again the truth in the assertion at 18:27

18.d   See 29:39. The three institutions/powers that comprised the fascist Egyptian regime and many other systems in history are referred by three characters: Pharaoh represents politics, Qarun represents economic monopoly, and Haman represents the military. What about magicians? Which institution/power do they represent? How do they contribute to the system that aims to accumulate power and wealth in the hands of the few? See 7:112-116; 28:38; 40:24-36.

19.c   For A, see 5:27-31; for B see 12:8-10; for C see 29:8-35; and for D see 45:16-17.

20.a   Salih is the only one that is not depicted as a Nabi (prophet).

Test 4

1.b   See 18:25. Through a unique expression, 300+9, God provides us with the period of their stay in the cave in both the solar and lunar calendars. Three hundred solar years corresponds to three hundred and nine lunar years. See 15:87 and 72:27

2.c   See 79:30. The Arabic word *dahaha* comes from root *dahy*, which means egg. The earth, with its physical shape and geologic layers resembles an egg. Though the roundness of the earth was known by philosophers before the revelation of the Quran, ordinary people did not find it a reasonable or common-sense fact. Therefore, almost all the commentators of the Quran tried to interpret the word so that they could save their flat earth from being curved. They reasoned that the verse must be an allegorical description, that God must have meant the nest or the place of the egg from the word egg. So, they translated this verse as follows: "and after that He spread the earth"!

3.b   See 11:62.

4.d   When the Quran uses the word *hadith* (word; saying; narration) for something other than itself, it usually uses it in negative way or context (7:185; 12:111; 31:6; 33:53; 45:6; 52:34; 66:3; 77:50). Since God knew that that Sunni and Shiite *mushriks* would create other authorities besides God in their religion and call them *hadith* and *sunna* of prophet Muhammad, the Quran uses the word *sunna* (law) too always with a negative meaning with the exception of those used in conjunction with God, as in "God's *sunna*" (33:38,62; 35:43; 40:85; 48:23). There is only one valid *sunna* (law, way) and it is God's *sunna*. Those who follow Muhammad's *sunna* or, more accurately, a man-made *sunna* falsely attributed to him, will be convicted to the *sunna* mentioned in 35:43. The singular word *sunna* is never used for other than God to denote a positive path; but its plural, *sunan*, is used once in a positive sense in connection to previous generations (4:26). More interesting, the third fabricated religious authority or idol is called *ijma* (consensus) and whenever this word or its derivatives are used in the Quran for other than God, they are always negative (20:60; 70:18; 104:2; 3:173; 3:157; 10:58; 43:32; 26:38; 12:15; 10:71; 20:64; 17:88; 22:73; 54:45; 28:78; 7:48; 26:39; 26:56; 54:44…). The same is true for the fourth word *sharia* (law) (42:21). The same is true for the word *salaf* (43:56) and for the word *ashaab* (53:2). Are all of these a coincidence? Since the followers of *hadith* and *sunna* do not translate these words, to expose the nature of their teachings we preferred not to translate some of those words too. This would not only expose their evil scheme, but would also highlight one of the prophetic features of the Quran. Faced with these prophetic Quranic challenges, later *Sunni* and *Shiite* scholars tried to hijack one of the attributes of the Quran, *hikma* (wisdom) or *hakim* (wise), for their *hadiths*; but they failed. The abundance of nonsense in *hadith* books did not accept or deserve such a description; they could not raise penguins in the middle of desert. See 6:112-116; 17:39; 36:1; 39:18; 66:3; 49:1; and 33:38.

5.c   Hoopoe delivered a message from Solomon to the Queen of Sheba. See 27:20-26

6.d   Numerical value of the Arabic letters comprising the word A1A1D4aM40 is 46, which is equal to the number of chromosomes in humans.

7.b   See 3:38-41; 19:7-15

8.c   See 33:37

9.a   See 19:29-30

10.c   See 33:13. Yathrib was the name of the city that Muhammad and his supporters immigrated to and there they established a constitutional federal system accommodating a multi-religious and multi-racial diverse population. But now we cannot find the name of Yathrib on the map. The followers of *hadith* and *sunna* changed the name of the city after Muhammad just as they changed many other things. Since *hadith* is the product of later generations who started calling Yathrib with the word *Medina* (City), Muslims abandoned the original name, the name that is mentioned in the Quran and was used by Muhammad and his companions. This is one of the many evidences that prove our assertion that "Muslims" have deserted the Quran and are following hearsay as their guide (25:30).

11.c   There are exactly 19 chapters with initial letters/numbers as independent verses. They are: 2, 3, 7, 19, 20, 26, 28, 29, 30, 31, 32, 36, 40, 41, 42, 43, 44, 45, 46.

12.d   The first chapter of the Quran has 7 verses, 29 words and 139 letters.

13.c   See 4:43. The followers of *hadith* and *sunna* reject the statement in the verse by claiming the presence of a contradiction between this verse and other verses prohibiting the intoxicants. Their rejection of God's verse and their allegation of contradiction in God's book are due to their ignorance of the fact that there could be individuals among muslims who consume alcoholic beverages just as there could be those who steal, commit adultery, or commit false accusation. Acknowledgement of the imperfect nature of a Muslim community does not mean that God justifies sins and crimes. Our Lord informs a Muslim who is doing wrong to himself or herself by consuming alcohol not to commit additional disrespect to God by addressing God in a drunken state of mind. Additionally, this verse indirectly gives permission to the community to not to allow their intoxicated brothers and sisters into the places of prostration. Another lesson derived from this commandment is that we should know what we are saying or reciting during our prayers. Reciting Arabic words without knowing their meanings is like praying while intoxicated. See 2:106; 4:82.

14.a   See 25:53. The water of lakes is maintained by rain. Through evaporation, the salty ocean water is filtered from its minerals. Evaporation creates a physical barrier between salty water and drinkable water.

15.b

16.a   See 2:69

17.d

18.d

19.d   See 42:52; 47:19; 48:2; and 93:7.

20.b   The Quran gives examples of many idolized concepts and objects. For instance, children (7:90), religious leaders and scholars (9:31), money and wealth (18:42), angels, dead saints, messengers and prophets (16:20,21; 35:14; 46:5,6; 53:23), and ego/wishful thinking (25:43, 45:23) all can be idolized.

Test 5

1.b   See 2:106. By declaring the word of God to be vague and ambiguous,
       early scholars opened the gate for unlimited abuse and distortion.
       Furthermore, by distorting the meaning of 2:106, they claimed that
       many verses of the Quran had been abrogated (amended) by other
       verses or *hadiths*. By this "abrogation theory," they amended verses
       which they did not understand, or which did not suit their interests, or
       which contradicted their *hadiths*. Repeating the same error committed
       by the Children of Israel (2:85), Muslims fulfilled the prophetic
       description of their action in 15:91-93. Some of them abrogated 5
       Quranic verses, some 20 verses and some 50.

       They support this claim by distorting the meaning of this verse. The
       Quran has a peculiar language. The word *Aya* in its singular form
       occurs 84 times in the Quran and in all cases, means miracle, evidence,
       or lesson. However, its plural form, *Ayat,* is used both for miracle,
       evidence, lesson, AND/OR for the language of the revelation that
       entails or leads to those miracles, evidences, and lessons. The fact that a
       verse of the Quran does not demonstrate the miraculous characteristics
       of the Quran supports this peculiar usage or vise versa. There are short
       verses that are comprised of only one or two words and they were most
       likely frequently used in daily conversation, letters and poetries. For
       instance, the verse "Where are you going?" cannot be called *AYAT*
       (signs) since it is one verse. This is very appropriate, since that
       expression was and is used by Arabic speaking people daily, even
       before the revelation of the Quran.

       However, in its semantic and numerical context, that short question is
       one of the *Ayat* of the Quran. See 55:3; 69:1; 74; 4; 75:8; 80:28; 81:26.
       Furthermore, we are informed that the minimum unit that demonstrates
       the Quran's miraculous nature is a chapter (10:38) and the shortest
       chapter consists of three verses (chapters 103, 108, and 110). The first
       verse of the Quran, commonly known as Basmala, though containing
       independent features, may not be considered a divine evidence/miracle
       on its own. However, it gains a miraculous nature with its numerical
       network with other letters, words, verses and chapters of the Quran. By
       not using the singular form *Aya* for the verses of the Quran, God also
       made it possible to distinguish the miracles shown in the language and
       prophecies of the scripture from the miracles shown in nature. See 4:82
       and 16:101 for further evidence that the Quranic verses do not abrogate
       each other.

       Since grammatically we can refer only to three verses with the plural
       word, *ayat,* and since we are not provided with a word to refer to a
       single or pair of verses, this unique use might have another implication:

are we required to quote the Quranic verses in segments of at least three verses? Will this method eliminate the abuse of Quranic statements by taking them out of their context? I think this question needs to be studied and tested. If quoting verses of the Quran in minimums of three units reasonably eliminates the abuse, then we should adhere to such a rule.

For another example of different meanings assigned to singular and plural forms of the same word, see 4:3. For a detailed discussion of this verse, see the Sample Comparisons section in the Introduction.

2.c   See 11:87. *Sala* prayer observed properly keeps away from immorality and crimes. See also 29:45.

3.c   See 17:36. This verse instructs us to use both our reason and senses to examine all the information we receive. It warns us against blindly following a religious teaching or political ideology and asks as to be iconoclasts. It warns us not to be hypnotized by the charisma of leaders nor by the social conventions. A society comprised of individuals that value rational and empirical inquiry will never become the victim of religious fanaticism, tragedies brought by charismatic politicians. A religion or sect that glorifies ignorance and gullibility can be very dangerous for its followers and others. As the Physicist Steven Weinberg once put profoundly, "With or without religion, you would have good people doing good things, and evil people doing evil things. But for good people to do evil things, that takes religion." See 6:74-83.

The Quran repeatedly advises us to use our intellect, to reason, to be open-minded, to be the seekers of truth, to be philosophers, to be critical thinkers, and not to be the followers of our wishful thinking or a particular crowd. For instance, see 2:170, 171, 242, 269; 3:118, 190; 6:74-83; 7:169; 8:22; 10:42, 100; 11:51; 12:2, 111; 13:4, 19; 16:67; 21:10, 67; 23:80; 24:61; 29:63; 30:28; 38:29; 39:9, 18, 21; 40:54; 59:14. See also 6:110.

4.d   In chapter 55, God asks us the following question exactly 31 times: "So which of your Lord's favors will you deny?"

5.a   The number/order of these chapters are: 11, 12, 13, 14, 15, 16.

6.a   See 3:18: "God bears witness that there is no god but He; as do the angels, and those with knowledge; He is standing with justice. There is no god but Him, the Noble, the Wise." The act of testifying to the oneness of God (*shahada*) is considered to be the essential requirement of being a Muslim. The expressions *la ilaha illa Allah* (there is no god, but the god) and *la ilaha illa Hu* (there is no god, but He) occur 30 times in the Quran and never in conjunction with another name. Trying a deficiency in the *shahada* taught by God is a sign of not valuing God as He should be valued. Requiring the addition of another name to God's name implies that God forgot to include Muhammad's name, thirty times (19:64; 6:115). Trying to teach God is the zenith of ignorance and audacity (49:16). Considering God alone insufficient is the symptom of idolatry (39:45).

7.b The four chapters are: 35 (Fatir/The Initiator), 40 (Ghafir/The Forgiver), 55 (Rahman/The Gracious), 87 (Al-A'la/The Most High),

8.a See 7:85

9.b As you might have suspected, this information is not given in the Quran. So, do not worry if you have missed it.

10.a See 2:247.

11.c See 29:14: "We had sent Noah to his people, so he stayed with them one thousand years less fifty calendar years. Then the flood took them while they were wicked." Until God revealed the secret code prophesied in chapter 74, we did not have a satisfactory answer to the question, why "one thousand minus fifty instead of the conventional expression, nine hundred and fifty?" Every element of the Quran, its chapters, verses, words, and letters, including its numbers, plays a role in the mathematical structure of the Quran. For instance, the sum of all the different numbers in the Quran without repetition gives us 162146 (19x8534). If the expression in the verse was "nine hundred and fifty," then the sum would be 900 extra and would not participate in the numerical system based on code 19. Furthermore, the age of Noah being a multiple of 19 also supports this relationship.

It seems too difficult to accept such a long lifespan for a human being. Since, the Quran contains its own scientific authentication; we have no choice but to trust this apparently incredible information.

12.d There are 38 un-initialed chapters between Chapter 2 and Chapter 68.

13.d The word *ahmad* in 61:6 is an adjective meaning "most acclaimed" or "most celebrated." Traditional sources consider it a proper name for Muhammad. This contradicts historical facts. The name of the prophet that came after Jesus was Muhammad, which is used in the Quran four times. Centuries after the departure of Muhammad, Muhammad-worshipers fabricated 99 names, including Ahmad, for Muhammad, in order to compete with the attributes of God. They could not accept one God having so many beautiful attributes, with their second god having only one attribute, Muhammad. They included many divine attributes, such as, "The First, The Last, The Judge.." in their list for Muhammad. Furthermore, we do not find the word Ahmad in the Bible. Rather we see the translation of the Greek adjective, "*paracletos*".

"And I will pray the Father, and he shall give you another Comforter/Counselor (*paracletus*), that he may abide with you for ever" (John 14:16). Also, see John 14:26; 15:26 16:7.

Jesus predicted the coming of another prophet. The one whose coming was foretold by Jesus is mentioned as "*Paracletos*" or "*Periclytos*" in Greek manuscripts. *Paracletos* means advocate, comforter, or counselor. *Periclytos*, on the other hand, means "admirable one" (in Arabic *ahmad*). The "spirit" here, does not mean other than human. There are cases where the word "spirit" is used for humans (2 Thessalonians 2:2; 1 John 4:1-3).

If indeed Jesus had prophesied the proper name of the prophet after him, this prophecy would have gotten the attention of almost every one of his supporters. Furthermore, we would see many people among his supporters and later Christians giving the name Ahmad to their sons, hoping that their sons would fulfill the prophecy. But, we do not even see a single Christian named Ahmad. Therefore, the Aramaic or Hebrew equivalent of this word did not become a name. However, the name Muhammad sharing the same root and similar meaning with the word *ahmad* is instructive.

14.d

15.a

16.d   See 15:87. The meaning of *saban minal mathani* (seven from pairs) has been interpreted by the majority of scholars as "oft-repeated seven," implying the most repeated chapter of the Quran, the seven-versed first chapter. However, if the first chapter of the Quran is part of the Quran, it surely is the part of the "great Quran." If the arrangement of the words were different, "we gave you the great Quran and seven from pairs," then, such an interpretation could be more plausible, since a part of the whole can be repeated after the whole for the purpose of emphasis. If the "great Quran" is the entire Quran, which is the most reasonable understanding, then the "seven pairs" or "fourteen" (of something) might have implications beyond the Quran. There is a hint in the verse: it might refer to the life span of Muhammad's people and its relation to the end of the world.

17.d   The order of revelation is not given by the Quran and the narrations are not reliable.

18.c   Lizard or gecko is not mentioned in the Quran. Interestingly hadith books are filled with hearsay reports attributed to Muhammad about eating or killing lizards/geckos. The Quran mentions numerous animals, each being witnesses to God's creative and intelligent design and signs, which started from a single cell: mosquito (2:26); calf

(2:51,54,92,93; 4:153; 7:148,152; 11:69; 20:88; 51:26); monkey (2:65; 5:60; 7:166); cow, heifer (2:67-71; 6:144,146; 12:43,46); pig (2:173; 5:3; 6:145; 16:115); donkey (2:259; 16:8; 31:19; 62:5); horse (3:14; 8:60; 16:8; 17:64; 59:6); falcon (5:4); dog, (5:4; 7:176; 18:18-22); crow (5:31); bird (6:38; 27:20); goat, sheep (6:143); camel (6:144; 88:17); adult he camel (7:40); she camel (7:73,77; 11:64; 17:59; 26:155; 54:27; 91:13); snake (7:107; 26:32), locust (7:133; 54:7); lice (7:133); frog (7:133); fish, whale (7:163; 18:61,63; 37:142; 68:48); wolf (12:17); bee (16:68); sheep/goat/ewe (20:18); fly (22:73); ant (27:18); hoopoe (27:20); spider (29:41); termite (34:14); ewe/sheep (38:23-24); lion (74:51); zebra (74:50); butterfly (101:4); elephant (105:1).

19.d

20.d   You might have noticed that we translated the reference of the verb *GHaLaBa* differently than the traditional translations. Instead of reading the verb in 30:2 as *ghulibat* (were defeated) we read as *ghalabat* which means just the opposite, "defeated." Similarly, we also read its continuous/future tense in the following verse differently. The prophecy of the verse was realized in 636, four years after the death of Muhammad, when Muslims confronted the army of Byzantine Empire around Yarmuk river, in one of the most significant battles in history. Under the command of Khalid bin Walid, the Muslim army beat the Christian imperial army of four or more times their numbers. The six-day war, Yarmuk, occurred in area near the Sea of Galilee and Dead Sea, which are located in the lowest land depression on earth, 200-400 meters below sea level.

The orthodox reading and translation of the verse, reflects an interesting historical conflict and is a prime example of the abuse of a divine book to justify nationalistic wars and imperialistic ambitions. By changing the verse's original reading to the opposite, the Umayyad and Abbasid dynasties were able to depict Persians as the major enemy. Thus, they justified aggression against Persian empire.

Test 6

1.a   The main problem comes from the word *iDRiBuhunne*, which has traditionally been translated as "beat them." The root of this word is *DaRaBa*. If you look at any Arabic dictionary, you will find a long list of meanings ascribed to this word. In fact, you will find that that list is one of the longest lists in your Arabic dictionary. It can be said that *DaRaBa* is the number-one multiple-meaning word in Arabic. It has so many different meanings; we can find numerous different meanings ascribed to it in the Quran.

2.a   Furthermore, note that we suggest REPARATION instead of Arabic word *jizya*. The meaning of *jizya* has been distorted as a tax on non-Muslims, which was invented long after Muhammad to further the imperialistic agenda of Kings. The origin of the word that we translated as Compensation is *JaZaYa*, which simply means compensation or, in the context of war, means war reparations, not tax. Since the enemies of Muslims attacked and aggressed, after the war they are required to compensate for the damage they inflicted on the peaceful community. Various derivatives of this word are used in the Quran frequently, and they are translated as compensation for a particular deed.

3.b   Traditional translations mistranslate the last three adjectives used here to describe Muslim women. They distort their meaning as "fasters, widows and virgins." When the issue is about women, somehow, the meaning of the Quranic words passes trough rapid mutations. For instance, we know that the Sunni and Shiite scholars who could not beat cows and examples found it convenient and fair to beat women (see 4:34). Those of us who have rejected other religious sources besides the Quran are still struggling to clean our minds from these innovations that even have sneaked into the Arabic language long after the revelation of the Quran. There is, in fact, nothing whatsoever about fasting, widows and virgins in this verse. We are rediscovering and relearning the Quran.

4.d   In this verse, the word *ummy* describes Meccan polytheists. It is obvious that *ummy* does not mean illiterate because it has been used as the counterpart of the people of the scripture. If the verse was " ... And say to those who are literate and illiterate," then the orthodox translation of *ummy* would be correct. According to 3:20, the people of the Arabian peninsula consisted of two main groups:

> The people of the scripture, i.e., Jews and Christians.
> Gentiles, who were neither Jewish nor Christian.

If the people who were neither Jews nor Christians were called *ummyyeen* (3:20; 3:75), then the meaning of *ummy* is very clear. As a matter of fact, the verse 3:75 clarifies its meaning as Gentile.

5.c

6.d

7.d

8.c   The Quran mentions communities as well as individuals who received retribution such as the People of Noah who were drowned for their intolerance for freedom of expression (26:105-122), the People of Thamud we were destroyed by an earthquake for oppressing the weak and their belligerence (7:7578; 11:61-68), the People of Lot for their sexual aggression and harassment (26:160-175), the People of Madyan or Woods who were annihilated by meteorites for their corrupt business affair (11:84-95; 26:176-191), Aad for indulging in vanity and supporting tyrants (11:59-60; 26:123-140), and the supporters of Pharaoh who were drowned for enslaving people and tyrannical rule (3:11; 11:96-99; 20:78-80; 26:10-68).

9.b   We know that during the era of Quranic revelation, Arabs were not using the so-called Arabic numerals. They adopted those numerals about two centuries after Muhammad. During the time of Muhammad, Arabs were using their Alphabet letters as numbers. The 28 letters of the Arabic alphabet then was arranged in a different order that started with the letters ABJD, thus known as *Abjad*, or Gematria. Since Arabic and Hebrew are closely related languages, their numerical system too resembled each other. Each letter corresponded to a number, such as A for 1, B for 2, J for 3, D for 4. When it reached 10, the corresponding numerical values would continue as multiples of tens and when reaching 100, they would continue as multiples of hundred ending with 1000. Archeological evidence shows that then they were distinguishing letters from numbers by using different color ink or simply by putting a line over the letter, resembling the Roman numerals. However, a literary text might use letters/numbers for multiple purposes; that is for both their semantic or lexicon function and at the same time for their numerical value. Such a multi-use requires an extreme command and knowledge of language and the author is limited by the language. When Arabs abandoned the *Abjad* system, it was still used by poets and charlatan healers who wished to take advantage of an antiquated numerical system that became a curiosity for the gullible. Poets wrote verses about events or epithets for important figures, with the date of the event or the death embedded in the numerical values of the letters of a word or a phrase in their verses. The usage of the *Abjad* in the

Quran is extensive, impressive and prophetic (For another example see 74:1-2).

10.a

11.d

12.c

13.c

14.d It is interesting that God informs us that Muhammad's only complaint will be about his people's desertion of the Quran (25:30). He will not complain that we deserted his *sunna*, as *hadith* books want us to believe. Those who are expecting their idol Muhammad to save them in the hereafter through his exclusive power of intercession will be surprised to witness rejection by their idols.

15.a According to 2:247, knowledge and health are two important characteristics needed for leadership. The expectation of wealth for appointed/elected leaders is criticized.

16.c The earth and heavenly bodies were once a single point and they were separated from each other (21:30). The universe is continuously expanding (51:47). Planet earth is floating in an orbit (27:88; 21:33; 36:40). The earth is round (10:24; 39:5; 55:33) and resembles an egg (10:24; 39:5; 79:30). The universe is also round (55:33). But, the Quran does not reject evolution. To the contrary, according to the Quran, the creation of living creatures follows an evolutionary system (7:69; 15:28-29; 24:45; 32:7-9; 71:14-17)

17.d See verse 7:156. The importance of *zaka*, purification/betterment through giving from blessings, is emphasized. *Infaq* is the financial *zaka*. The amount of financial charity (2:219; 17:26, 29), its time (6:141), the list of recommended recipients (2:215), how it will be given (2:274; 13:22), and why it should be given (30:39) are all clarified.

18.d

19.g,h,i The last three translations are the accurate rendering of original. Those who do not know Arabic might think that the words are difficult to understand and translate. In fact, the meaning of these two words, *LaWwaHa* and *BaSHaR* is very clear in the Quranic context. The word *LaWwaHa*, which comes from the root *LWH*, is the sister of the word *LaWH* (85:22) and its plural *aLWaH*. The plural form *aLWaH* is used in verses 7:145, 150, 154 for the "tablets" given to Moses, and in verse 54:13 for broad planks used by Noah to build his ark. The medieval commentators, not knowing the mathematical implication of the verses, mostly chose an unusual meaning for the word: scorching, burning, shriveling, etc. Ironically, most of them did acknowledge the obvious meaning of the word as "open board, tablet" (See Baydawi, Fakhruddin Al-Razi, etc.). Few preferred the "obvious" to the obscure. For instance, Muhammad Asad, who had no idea of the mathematical code, preferred the most obvious meaning. Rashad Khalifa who fulfilled the prophecy and discovered the implication of the entire chapter reflected the same obvious meaning. That "obvious" meaning was obscured by the smoke of "scorching fire" burning in the imaginations of generations before him.

In 7:145; 7:150; 7:154, the word *aLWaH*, the plural of *LaWHa* is used to depict the tablets on which the Ten Commandments were inscribed. In 54:13 it is used to describe the structure of the Noah's ship made of wood panes. In 85:22 the same word is used for the mathematically protected record of the original version of the Quran. As for the *LaWaHa* of 74:29, it is the amplified noun-adjective derived from the root of the verb LWH, meaning open tablets, succeeding screens, obvious, manifesto, or clearly and perpetually visible. Ironically, the Quran uses different words to describe burning or scorching. For instance, for burning, the derivatives of *HaRaQa* (2:266; 3:181; 7:5; 20:97; 21:68; 22:9; 22:22; 29:24; 75:10), or for scorching the derivatives of *SaLaYa* (4:10; 4:30; 4:56; 4:115; 14:29; 17:18; 19:70; 27:7; 28:29; 29:31; 36:64; 38:56; 38:59; 38:163; 52:16; 56:94; 58:8; 69:31; 74: 26; 82:15; 83:16; 84:12; 87:12; 88:12; 92:15), or *NaDaJa* are used (4:56).

Again, we should note that the understanding of pre-1974 commentators was not without basis. Though their understanding did not rely on the Quranic usage of the words, and created some problems (such as explaining the verse 74:31), they had some justifiable excuses to understand the way they understood. The word *LaWaHa* also meant burn and *BaSHaRa* was another word for skin in Arabic language. As I mentioned above, the multiple meanings of these verses allowed the impatient pre-1974 generations to have an understanding, though a temporary and not primarily intended one. In fact, it was better for them to have patience and not rush to speculate on these verses without knowledge (20:114; 75:16-19). See (10:37-46).

20. c Putting the eggs in different baskets is one of the ways of risk management.

61

Theometer or Sectometer

(First conducted on the participants of my lectures at Oxford University in November 3-5, 2008)

Edip Yuksel

Name: _____

Email Address: _____

Phone: _____ Age: _____

Occupation: _____

Nationality: _____

Have you read the Manifesto for Islamic Reform? _____

Favorite Books/Authors: _____

Your Sect: (a) Sunni (b) Shiite (c) Salafi (d) Other (d) No sect

Please put a CIRCLE around the letter of your choice:

1. According to the Quran, which one of these is not and cannot be idolized by people?

    a. Prophet Muhammad
    b. Desires or Wishful thinking (Hawa)
    c. Crowds or peers
    d. Ancestors or children
    e. Reasoning (Aql)

2. Which one of these is a true statement?

    a. The Quran is not sufficient to guide us; in addition we need Hadith and Sunna.
    b. The Quran is not sufficient to guide us; we need Hadith, Sunna and follow the teaching of a Sunni sect.
    c. The Quran is not sufficient to guide us; we need Hadith, Sunna and follow the teaching of a Shiite sect.
    d. The Quran is not sufficient to guide us; we need Hadith, Sunna, follow the teaching of a sect and join a religious order.
    e. The Quran is sufficient to guide us when we understand and follow it through the light of reason.

3. Which one of these hadiths narrated by Bukhari, Muslim and other "authentic" hadith books, do you think are fabricated:

    a. Muhammad was illiterate until he died.
    b. Muhammad married Aisha at age 54 while she was only 9 or 13 years-old.
    c. Muhammad dispatched a gang of fighters (sariyya) to kill a woman poet secretly during night in her home, for criticizing him publicly through her poems.
    d. Muhammad slaughtered 400 to 900 Jews belonging to Ben Qurayza for violating the treaty.
    e. All of the above.

4. Which one of these laws or rules does not exist in the Quran?

    a. Stone the married adulterers to death
    b. Do not play guitar
    c. Men should not wear silk and gold
    d. Men are superior to women
    e. All of the above

5. The Quran instructs us to follow the messengers. Following the messenger means:

    a. Follow Hadith and Sunna; Bukhari, Muslim, Ibn Hanbal, etc.
    b. Follow his Ahl-al-Bayt.
    c. Follow hadith, sunna, consensus of sahaba, ijtihad of imams and fatwas of ulama.
    d. Follow Muhammad.
    e. Follow the message he was sent with, which was Quran alone.

6. The Quran is God's word, because:
    a.   There are verses of the Quran stating that it is God's word.
    b.   The Quran is a literary miracle. None can bring a sura like it surpassing its literary qualities.
    c.   I do not need to have a reason. Reason is not reliable. I have faith in the Quran.
    d.   The moral teaching of the Quran is the best for individual and humanity.
    e.   The Quranic signs (aya) do not have internal contradiction nor does it contradict the signs in nature. Besides, it is numerically coded book with an extraordinary mathematical structure integrated with its composition and Arabic language.

7. Which one of the following is correct for Muhammad:
    a.   Muhammad was the final messenger and prophet.
    b.   Muhammad had the highest rank above all humans.
    c.   Muhammad demonstrated many miracles such as splitting the moon, healing the sick, and crippling a child
    d.   All of the above´
    e.   Muhammad was a human messenger like other messengers.

8. In what year he Bukhari started collecting hadith for his hadith collection known as the Sahih Bukhari, the most trusted Sunni hadith collection?
    a.   During the life of Muhammad in Medina
    b.   Ten years after Muhammad's death.
    c.   130 years after Muhammad's death.
    d.   200 years after Muhammad's death
    e.   230 years after Muhammad's death.

9. According to Bukhari himself, he collected the 7,275 hadith among the 700,000 hadiths he collected. If each hadith, together with its *isnad* (the chain of reporters) and *sanad* (the text that was attributed to Muhammad) took about half a book page, how many volumes of books with 500 pages would they take to record all those 700,000 hadith allegedly collected by Bukhari?
    a.   7 volumes

    b.   10 volumes
    c.   70 volumes
    d.   100 volumes
    e.   700 volumes

10. What are the last statements in the Farewell Sermon (Khutba al-Wida) which was reportedly witnessed by more than 100,000 sahaba, making it by far the most authentic hadith among the thousands of hadiths?
    a.   I leave you Abu Bakr; you should follow him.
    b.   I leave you my sahaba; you may follow any of them.
    c.   I leave you the Quran and Sunna; you should follow both.
    d.   I leave you the Quran and Ahl-al-Bayt (my family); you should follow them.
    e.   I leave you the Quran, you should follow it.

11. According to some "authentic hadith" found in Bukhari and other hadith books, there was a verse instructing muslims to stone the married adulterers to death: "Al-shayhu wal-shayhatu iza zanaya farjumuhuma nakalan..." According to hadith reports, what happened to those verses?
    a.   After the Prophet Muhammad's death, Umayyad governor Marwan burned the pages where those verses were written.
    b.   Angle Gebrail came down and deleted it from the scripture.
    c.   Ibni Abbas forgot it yet Abu Hurayra never forgot it.
    d.   There is no reference to such a verse in any authentic hadith books.
    e.   After the Prophet Muhammad's death, the skin which the verse was written on was protected under Aisha's bed. A hungry goat ate it. Thus, it was abrogated literally yet kept legally.

12. According to both Bukhari and Muslim, when Muhammad was in his death bed, he asked his comrades around to bring him a paper and pen to write something for them so that they would not divert from the right path. According to the same "authentic" Sunni hadith books, Omar bin Khattab stopped a sahaba who was hurrying for a paper and pen and said the following: "The prophet is sick and has fever. He does not know what he is

saying. God's book is sufficient for us."
According to the hadith, all the prominent
comrades (sahaba) agreed with Omar and
Muhammad passed away without writing
down his advice. What do you think about this
hadith?

   a. If it is narrated by both Bukhari and
       Muslim, then it must be true
   b. If it is true, then, Omar and all other
       Sahaba must have betrayed
       Muhammad and committed
       blasphemy.
   c. If it is true, then, Omar and all
       prominent Sahaba were followers
       of the Quran alone.
   d. If it is false then all other hadith too
       should be rejected.
   e. C and D must be true

13. Do we need to SAY *sallallahu alayhi
wasallam* after Muhammad's name?

   a. Yes, every time Muhammad is
       mentioned we have to praise his
       name.
   b. Yes, but we need to say only once
       in our lifetime.
   c. Yes, the more we say the better.
   d. Yes, and those who do not say it
       after Muhammad's name disrespect
       him and they will not receive his
       intercession.
   e. No, the Quran does not ask us to
       say anything after Muhammad's
       name; muslims were asked (salli
       ala) to support him, as he was also
       asked to support them (salli
       alayhim).

14. What is the correct Testimony (*shahada*)
according to the Quran:

   a. I bear witness that there is no god
       but the God and the Quran is God's
       word.
   b. I bear witness that there is no god
       but the God and Muhammad is His
       messenger.
   c. I bear witness that there is no god
       but the God and Muhammad is His
       messenger and His servant.
   d. I bear witness that there is no god
       but the God and Abraham, Jesus,
       Moses and Muhammad are His
       messengers.
   e. I bear witness that there is no god
       but the God.

15. Should Muslims who do not observe
daily prayers be beaten in public?
   a. Yes.
   b. No.

16. Should Muslims who are caught for
consuming alcohol for the fourth time be
killed?
   a. Yes.
   b. No.

17. Did the prophet give permission to kill
women and children in the war?
   a. Yes.
   b. No.

18. According to the Quran, are women
banned from reading Quran and pray during
their menstruation periods?
   a. Yes
   b. No.

19. In the daily Sala prayers, do you recite
*attahiyyatu lillahi wassalawatu .... as salamu
alayka ayyuhannabiyyu wa rahmatullahi wa
barakatuhu*?
   a. Yes
   b. No

20. Does the Quran justify taxing Jewish and
Christian population under Muslim authority
with extra or different taxation called Jizya?
   a. Yes
   b. No.

21. Does the Quran instruct women to cover
their hair?
   a. Yes.
   b. No.

22. Are woman restricted from leading
congregational prayers?
   a. Yes.
   b. No.

23. Are women mentally and spiritually
inferior to men?
   a. Yes.
   b. No.

24. Does the Quran restrict women from
initiating divorce?
   a. Yes.
   b. No.

25. Is polygamy with previously unmarried women allowed?
- a. Yes, up to four women.
- b. No, polygamy is allowed only with the widows who have orphans.

26. Do pilgrims need to cast real stones at the devil?
- a. Yes.
- b. No.

27. Is the black stone near Kaba holy?
- a. Yes.
- b. No.

28. May a muslim own slaves?
- a. Yes.
- b. No.

29. Is circumcision a required or encouraged practice in Islam?
- a. Yes.
- b. No.

30. Should converts change their names to Arabic names?
- a. Yes.
- b. No.

31. How much *zaka* charity one should give away?
- a. 2.5%
- b. As much as one can afford, without making themselves needy.

32. Are those who break their fast during Ramadan before the sunset required to fast 60 consecutive days as a punishment for not completing the day?
- a. Yes.
- b. No.

33. Is leadership the right of Quraish tribe?
- a. Yes.
- b. No.

34. Is drawing pictures or making three dimensional statutes a sin?
- a. Yes.
- b. No.

35. Are there more dietary prohibitions besides pork, carcass, running blood, and animal dedicated to idolized names?
- a. Yes.
- b. No.

36. Is displaying Muhammad's name and the names of his closest companions next to God's name in the mosques idol-worship?
- a. Yes.
- b. No.

37. Did Muhammad advise some sick people to drink camel urine?
- a. Yes.
- b. No.

38. Did Muhammad gauge people's eyes with hot nails?
- a. Yes.
- b. No.

39. After following the advice of Moses, did Muhammad, bargain with God about the number of prayers, lowering down from the impossible-to-observe 50 times a day to 5 times a day?
- a. Yes.
- b. No.

40. Does Muhammad have the power of intercession?
- a. Yes.
- b. No.

41. Was Muhammad sinless?
- a. Yes.
- b. No.

42. Did God create the universe for the sake of Muhammad?
- a. Yes.
- b. No.

43. Did Muhammad have sexual power of 30 males?
- a. Yes.
- b. No.

44. Was Muhammad bewitched by a Jew?
- a. Yes.
- b. No.

45. Do some verses of the Quran abrogate other verses?
- a. Yes.
- b. No.

Here is the story and the answer of this test:

Between November 3 and 10 of 2008, I traveled to UK and Turkey to deliver four lectures; first two at Oxford University, the third at Muslim Institute in London and the fourth one in Istanbul Book Fair. I had prepared a test containing 45 multiple choice questions just the night before my travel. I duplicated them on both sides of a single sheet and I distributed to the audience before the lecture... They were asked to write their name, age, occupation, email address, favorite authors, and their sectarian affiliation. It was a bit awkward to test an audience that consisted of students and professors at one of the world's top universities. The multiple-choice test proved to be a powerful instrument to deliver the message of Islamic Reform under the light of the Quran. The correct answer for each multiple choice question was the E option, and for the Yes or No questions was the B option. So, it would take me a few seconds to evaluate the tests after they were returned to me.

The Sunni or Shiite test-takers found themselves in quagmire of contradiction with their own sectarian teachings. They learned that they were thirty, forty or even more than fifty percent infidels or heretics. Some of those who marked Sunni as their sectarian affiliation contradicted the Sunni teachings on most of the issues. According to their own confessed sects, their lives were worthless; they deserved to be killed! I did not let this mirror or sect-o-meter remain an individual experience; I publicly declared the overall results. Many got all answers correct, including Eric, a monotheist from Unitarian church who already had a copy of the Quran: a Reformist Translation in his possession. Eric knew the original message of islam better than all the mullahs and the so-called "ulama" combined.

If you have chosen the wrong option for any of the questions and you are wondering why you have contradicted the Quran, please visit **www.islamicreform.org** and read the full version of the Manifesto for Islamic Reform. If you prefer to have it in a book form, you may order it by visiting **www.brainbowpress.com**

Rules to Understand the Quran

F.K.[1]

(Dear Edip. The Quran as a guiding book has its own guidance about itself. It defines itself, and shows ways to consider reading it for best understanding. I have extracted 19 rules that one can follow. Also I would like to mention that I did not try to purposely discover 19 rules. It just happened. You may classify them differently if you want to. This is not ready for publication, but if you wish you may improve and publish it under your name.)

Rule 1: Do not abandon the Quran. Verse 25:30 is clear about that. From this verse we must conclude that the reading of The Quran is an obligation. It is *Fardh* as they say in Arabic. The Quran did not leave room for too much speculation about this rule. Verses 28:85 and 24:1 are further clarifications. Please read those verses and think about it.

Rule 2: It is easy to understand. Be sure that it is easy to understand. The divine reminder in 54:17 is repeated four times in chapter 54. It is easy. If you say it is difficult, indeed it becomes difficult. First, because you rejected God's repeated assertions about the Quran, and second, because of this prejudice you lost all the motivation and wits to understand even the simplest statements. Therefore, you must read it to understand and think about it. The Quran makes it clear that the messenger will not spoonfeed it to people. They have to figure it out on their own (38:29).

Rule 3: Best times to read it. You can read the Quran anytime that is possible for you. Read and reflect on it at nights. The best time for most benefit is early morning (17:78). When your mind is clean and ready to take in.

Rule 4: Trust it and be free of doubts on its authenticity. Trust it. It will clear out your questions and concerns (5:101). God's book is safe. No one can fabricate it and mess with it (10:37). Read it with no concern.

---

[1] F.K. is a Kurdish-American (born in Iraq) monotheist with dozens of patents in computer hardware technology. He has a PhD in mathematics.

Rule 5: Be unbiased. Don't read it when you are biased with pre-established position. Be clean from your ego. Make sure you are not reading for your personal gains against it, or for it, or just use for manipulating others. The Quran makes it clear that it will be difficult or impossible for unclean to get in touch with it. See, 56:79. Yes, of course it is difficult to be clean from ego and hidden agendas. But, you must try your best. That is the reason why the Quran asks you to seek refuge to God whenever you read The Quran (16:98). You do not need to "say" some words, but you must think about it. Once you are neutral and have a clean heart, the Quran opens up to you. In another words, your mind opens up to the Quran.

Rule 6: Listen to it whenever it is recited (7:204). You don't have to think about it and study it only when you yourself reading it. Sometimes when others read it, your mind will be free and can comprehend it much better.

Rule 7: Good reading, good habit of reading is necessary. Make sure you pay attention to it. Many people read books while their minds are not even there. Their lips move and sounds come out. Engage the verses with each other to close the gap in your understanding. Organize the verses well (73:4). Remember, the Quran is not organized in its chronological chain. This shows the flexibility for organizing in various studies as you see in this research. This leads you to be mentally active, not a passive follower of a good story.

Rule 8: Make sure do not mix cultural practices with the Quran (5:104). We learn things through culture and we think it is part of the Quran. Be careful not to reject the Quran because of the differences you see in norms.

Rule 9: It does not make your life miserable. Remember this Quran did not come to you to make your life miserable (20:2). It should drive you toward easy and happy life (87:8). The Quran leads you to be in peace with your intellect and nature. So if you find implementing certain verses makes your life miserable be sure that you do not have an understanding of its meaning. Stop there and re-read that verse and study it again according to all the rules until it clears out. The Quran is supposed to make your life good here and hereafter. This is a good rule to follow to understand the Quran.

Rule 10: Do not chop it. Do not chop or cut the verses. It is not fair to cut a verse and then use it for ill intentions. This is a bad manner and is not acceptable in any norm. You can't take a half sentence from one and use it against him/her (15:89-91). Make sure no one misleads and manipulate you and others through this common abuse of the Quran.

Rule 11: It is a complete universe. The Quran is detailed and its verses are packed together in a very intelligent way. As the planets and the stars are having effect on each other, the verses are the same. You can't understand a verse in isolation from rest of the book. Do not rush to reach conclusions until you see the entire the Quran (20:114) (Why verse number 114? Amazing ☺). Once you see all the Quran and related verses to the subject verse, you will understand it better.

Rule 12: No contradiction in the Quran (4:82). This rule is very useful to give the reader a tool to clarify his understanding. Once you find a verse contradicts another one, you must stop at once with no conclusion. Back up and try to question every word, every verse until you reach a consistent understanding. God will not contradict himself. Many Muslim scholars made mistakes by ignoring this rule. For instance the verse 2:62 and 3:19 may look contradictory to each other on the surface. This caused great misunderstanding among Muslims. But, a careful debugging and verification of the word Islam will show that there is no contradiction. Once you clear that you understand the Quran better. It is great rule for verification and in depth understanding.

Rule 13: God teaches the Quran (55:2). Once you find yourself having difficulties understanding the true meaning of verse of a word, go through the entire Quran searching for that word and its uses in various forms in various verses. You will start getting clearer understanding slowly. God repeats some phrases and words for many reasons. One of the reasons is to teach us the true meanings. There are other ways but you must experience it on your own.

Rule 14: Use resources, including the Torah and Injeel (3:2, 4:36, 5:69, 4:135, 5:67). It is useful sometimes to look at these sources to understand better. But, be cautious. Also use specialists by asking them. Do searches through media.

Rule 15: The Quran is not a magic book. It is important to understand the Quran as a guiding book and not a machine to change people. God has given us the freedom of choice and He will not force people and does not allow any one use force (17:41; 2:256).

Rule 16: There are fixed verses and there are allegorical and multi-meaning ones (3:7). Make sure you pay special attention to those allegorical or multi-meaning verses. People can manipulate them. They require special reading and knowledge to follow them. If you can't, don't worry. They have their meanings planted in other verses. You will not miss their benefits.

Rule 17: Do not reject because you do not understand. Many people reject some verses of the Quran or any book if they do not understand them. Many years ago, if one said hands and legs will witness against people it would have been rejected (24:23). These days we know we can use lie detectors by monitoring skin, hand, face and so on. This knowledge is new. Imagine what we could do in a 1000 years from now. So do not reject things you do not understand. Ignorance does not prove nor disprove anything (10:39).

Rule 18: Group Study. Group study is a proven method to help understand, discover, and come to better understanding. When organizations want to find new fresh ideas and better understanding of issues, they perform brain-storming, which is done in group meetings. The Quran advices us to use group study whenever we reach a point were we can not understand it. See 34: 44-45. I think this method is useful even if you have an understanding so you find out if you make any sense

Rule 19: The Quran is a unique and interesting book, filled with prophecies and signs. If you do not follow the crowds, your peers or your ancestors blindly and if you search for truth continuously as it is instructed by the Quran (17:36), God will show His signs in your person and in the horizons (41:53). If you belong to the group that appreciate the Quran's prophetic sign (74:31) and became one of those who are described "progressive" (74.37), you are in minority. Against ignorant and arrogant people, be patient, and follow verse 39:18.

No Contradiction in the Quran

Verse 4:82 of the Quran claims that the book remains free of contradictions. Any internal contradictions between the Quran and God's laws in nature falsifies the claim. I found the following claims for contradictions posted on an evangelical site disguised as "humanist." Below, you will find the 10 charges with my answers.

QUESTION 1: What was man created from — blood, clay, dust, or nothing?

1. "Created man, out of a (mere) clot of congealed blood," (96:2).

2. "We created man from sounding clay, from mud molded into shape, (15:26).

3. "The similitude of Jesus before Allah is as that of Adam; He created him from dust, then said to him: "Be". And he was," (3:59).

4. "But does not man call to mind that We created him before out of nothing?" (19:67, Yusuf Ali). Also, 52:35).

5. "He has created man from a sperm-drop; and behold this same (man) becomes an open disputer! (16:4).

ANSWER 1: Human beings were created from earthly materials and water according to divinely guided evolution.

The criticism presented above serves as a classic example of an EITHER-OR fallacy, or the product of a mind that does not consider or perceive time and evolution as reality. If he uses the same standards, the critic of these verses will find contradictions in almost every book. If he looks into biology books, he will similarly get confused. In one page he will learn that he is made of atoms, in another cells, in another DNA, and sperm, egg, embryo, earthly materials, etc. He would express his disbelief and confusion with a similar question. A careful and educated reading of the Quran reveals the following facts about creation:

1. There were times when man did not exist. Billions of years after the creation of the universe, humans were created. In other words, we were nothing before we were created:

"Did the human being forget that we created him already, and he was nothing?" (19:67).

71

2. Humans were created according to divinely guided evolution:

"Have they not seen how GOD initiates the creation, and then repeats it? This is easy for GOD to do. Say, 'Roam the earth and find out the origin of life.' For GOD will thus initiate the creation in the Hereafter. GOD is Omnipotent." (29:19-20).

"He is the One who created you in stages. Do you not realize that GOD created seven universes in layers? He designed the moon therein to be a light, and placed the sun to be a lamp And GOD germinated you from the earth like plants." (71:14-17).

3. Creation of man started from clay:

"We created the human being from aged mud, like the potter's clay." (15:26).

Our Creator began the biological evolution of microscopic organisms within the layers of clay. Donald E. Ingber, professor atHarvard University, published an article titled "The Architecture of Life" as the cover story of Scientific American. He stated the following:

"Researchers now think biological evolution began in layers of clay, rather than in the primordial sea. Interestingly, clay is itself a porous network of atoms arranged geodesically within octahedral and tetrahedral forms. But because these octahedra and tetrahedra are not closely packed, they retain the ability to move and slide relative to one another. This flexibility apparently allows clay to catalyze many chemical reactions, including ones that may have produced the first molecular building blocks of organic life."

Humans are advanced fruits of organic creation, initiated millions of years ago from layers of clay.

4. Human beings are made of water:

"Do the unbelievers not realize that the heaven and the earth used to be one solid mass that we exploded into existence? And from water we made all living things. Would they believe?" (21:30).

The verse above not only emphasizes the importance of water as an essential ingredient for organic life, it also clearly refers to the beginning of the universe, or what we now call the Big Bang. The Quran's information regarding cosmology remains centuries ahead of its time. For instance, verse 51:47 informs us that the universe is continuously expanding. "We constructed the sky with our hands, and we will continue to expand it." Furthermore, the Quran informs us that the universe will collapse back to its origin, confirming the closed-universe model: "On that day, we will fold the heaven, like the folding of a book. Just as we initiated the first creation, we will repeat it. This is our promise; we will certainly carry it out." (21:104).

"And GOD created every living creature from water. Some of them walk on their bellies, some walk on two legs, and some walk on four. GOD creates whatever He wills. GOD is Omnipotent." (24:45).

Bipedal motion on two legs serves as a crucial point in the evolution of humanoids. Walking on two feet may initially appear to be insignificant in the evolutionary process, but many scientists believe that walking on two feet made significant contributions to human evolution by enabling Homo Erectus to use tools and gain consciousness, thereby leading to Homo Sapiens.

4. Human beings are made of dust, or earth, containing essential elements for life:

"The example of Jesus, as far as GOD is concerned, is the same as that of Adam; He created him from dust, then said to him, "Be," and he was." (3:59).

5. Human beings are the product of long-term evolution, and when human sperm and egg, consisting of water and earthly elements, meet each other in the right condition, they evolve to the embryo, the fetus, and finally after 266 days, into a human being:

"Was he not a drop of ejected semen?" (75:37).

"He created the human from a tiny drop, and then he turns into an ardent opponent." (16:4).

"He created man from an embryo." (96:2).

" O people, if you have any doubt about resurrection, (remember that) we created you from dust, and subsequently from a tiny drop, which turns into a hanging (embryo), then it becomes a fetus that is given life or deemed lifeless. We thus clarify things for you. We settle in the wombs whatever we will for a predetermined period. We then bring you out as infants, then you reach maturity. While some of you die young, others live to the worst age, only to find out that no more knowledge can be attained beyond a certain limit. Also, you look at a land that is dead, then as soon as we shower it with water, it vibrates with life and grows all kinds of beautiful plants." (22:5).

As you noticed, we do not translate the Arabic word "Alaq" as "clot." Since neither in interspecies evolution nor in intraspecies evolution does a stage exist where human beings are clots, this is a traditional mistranslation of the word, and the error was first noticed by medical doctor Maurice Bucaille. Any decent Arabic dictionary will give you three definitions for the word "Alaq" — (1) clot;

(2) hanging thing; (3) leech. Early commentators of the Quran, lacking the knowledge of embryology, justifiably picked the "clot" as the meaning of the word. However, the author of the Quran referred to the embryo through this multiple-meaning word, as it hangs to the wall of the uterus and nourishes itself like a leech. In modern times, we do not have an excuse for picking the wrong meaning. This is one of the many examples of the Quran's language in verses related to science and mathematics. While its words provide understanding to former generations, its real meaning shines with knowledge of God's creation and natural laws.

QUESTION 2: Is there or is there not compulsion in religion according to the Qur'an?

1. "Let there be no compulsion in religion: Truth stands out clear from Error: whoever rejects evil and believes in Allah hath grasped the most trustworthy hand-hold, that never breaks. And Allah heareth and knoweth all things," (2:256).

2. "And an announcement from Allah and His Messenger, to the people (assembled) on the day of the Great Pilgrimage,- that Allah and His Messenger dissolve (treaty) obligations with the Pagans. If then, ye repent, it were best for you; but if ye turn away, know ye that ye cannot frustrate Allah. And proclaim a grievous penalty to those who reject Faith," (9:3).

3. "But when the forbidden months are past, then fight and slay the Pagans wherever ye find them, and seize them, beleaguer them, and lie in wait for them in every stratagem (of war); but if they repent, and establish regular prayers and practice regular charity, then open the way for them: for Allah is Oft-forgiving, Most Merciful," (9:5). "Fight those who believe not in Allah nor the Last Day, nor hold that forbidden which hath been forbidden by Allah and His Messenger, nor acknowledge the religion of Truth, (even if they are) of the People of the Book, until they pay the Jizya with willing submission, and feel themselves subdued," (9:29).

ANSWER 2: Yes, there is no compulsion in religion according to the Quran, and Muslims are permitted to defend themselves against aggressors and murderers.

The Quran promotes freedom of opinion, religion, and expression. The critic takes the verses from Chapter 9 out of context and presents them as a contradiction with the principle expressed in 2:256 and other verses. Chapter 9 starts with an ultimatum for Meccan mushriks who tortured, killed, and evicted muslims from their homes, and who also mobilized several major war campaigns against them while they established a peaceful multinational and multi-religious community. The beginning of the chapter refers to their violation

74

of the peace treaty and provides them with an ultimatum and four months to stop the aggression. Thus, the verses quoted from Chapter 9 have nothing to do with freedom of religion. They are a warning against aggressive and murderous fanatics.

I discussed this subject extensively in my first debate, and I argued that Sunni tyrants distorted the meaning of the word JIZYA as a taxation against non-muslims, while the word more accurately means "compensation" or "war reparations" which were was levied against the aggressor parties that initiated the war. My argument on Quran's position regarding war and peace is posted at the Articles section of 19.org under the title "To the Factor of 666."

QUESTION 3: The first Muslim was Muhammad? Abraham? Jacob? Moses?

1. "And I [Muhammad] am commanded to be the first of those who bow to Allah in Islam," (39:12).

2. "When Moses came to the place appointed by Us, and his Lord addressed him, He said: "O my Lord! show (Thyself) to me, that I may look upon thee." Allah said: "By no means canst thou see Me (direct); But look upon the mount; if it abide in its place, then shalt thou see Me." When his Lord manifested His glory on the Mount, He made it as dust. And Moses fell down in a swoon. When he recovered his senses he said: "Glory be to Thee! to Thee I turn in repentance, and I am the first to believe." (7:143).

3. "And this was the legacy that Abraham left to his sons, and so did Jacob; "Oh my sons! Allah hath chosen the Faith for you; then die not except in the Faith of Islam," (2:132).

ANSWER 3: Many prophets and messengers were the first muslims in their time and location.

If we check Google.com with the search tag "Olympic first place 100-meters + running," we will find many names for athletes who received first place. If we use the critic's logic, we would think that great confusion and contradictory claims exist regarding the first-place winner for the 100-meter race. What is wrong with that logic? Obviously, we need to consider time and space! Abraham was first muslim (submitter and promoter of peace) in his time and location. Similarly, Moses and Muhammad were also pioneer muslims in their times.

QUESTION 4: Does Allah forgive or not forgive those who worship false gods?

1 "Allah forgiveth not that partners should be set up with Him; but He forgiveth anything else, to whom He pleaseth; to set up partners with Allah is to devise a sin Most heinous indeed," (4:48 ; Also 4:116).

2 "The people of the Book ask thee to cause a book to descend to them from heaven: Indeed they asked Moses for an even greater (miracle), for they said: "Show us Allah in public," but they were dazed for their presumption, with thunder and lightning. Yet they worshipped the calf even after clear signs had come to them; even so we forgave them; and gave Moses manifest proofs of authority," (4:153).

ANSWER 4: God does not forgive those who associate other powers or gods to Him, if they do not repent on time.

The Quran contains numerous verses regarding idol-worshipers or mushriks accepting the message of islam.

"He is the One who accepts the repentance from His servants, and remits the sins. He is fully aware of everything you do." (42:25).

Most supporters and companions of messengers and prophets associated partners to God before they repented and accepted the message. For instance, the Quran informs us that Muhammad was a polytheist before he received revelation, but after his acknowledgement of the truth he repented regarding his ignorance and God forgave him.

"Say, 'I have been enjoined from worshiping the idols you worship beside GOD, when the clear revelations came to me from my Lord. I was commanded to submit to the Lord of the universe.'" (40:66).

"Thus, we inspired to you a revelation proclaiming our commandments. You had no idea about the scripture, or faith. Yet, we made this a beacon to guide whomever we choose from among our servants. Surely, you guide in a straight path." (42:52).

"He found you astray, and guided you." (93:7).

"Whereby GOD forgives your past sins, as well as future sins, and perfects His blessings upon you, and guides you in a straight path." (48:2).

QUESTION 5: Are Allah's decrees changed or not?

1. "Rejected were the messengers before thee: with patience and constancy they bore their rejection and their wrongs, until Our aid did reach them: there is none

76

that can alter the words (and decrees) of Allah. Already hast thou received some account of those messengers," (6:34).

2. "The word of thy Lord doth find its fulfillment in truth and in justice: None can change His words: for He is the one who heareth and knoweth all, (6:115).

3. "None of Our revelations do We abrogate or cause to be forgotten, but We substitute something better or similar: Knowest thou not that Allah Hath power over all things?" (2:106).

4. "When We substitute one revelation for another,- and Allah knows best what He reveals (in stages),- they say, "Thou art but a forger": but most of them understand not," (16:101).

ANSWER 5: God's decrees do not change.

This is a valid criticism against those who do not follow the Quran alone, since they have distorted the meaning of 2:106 and 16:101 through fabricated hadiths. Quran's definition of "does not change" refers to *Sunnatullah* (God's law) and *Kalimatullah* (God's word), as in 6:34 and 6:115. Verses 2:106 and 16:101 contain neither of these words; they describe God's AYAT (Sign; miracle) given to prophets and messengers. The translation the critic uses contains a translation error, with grave theological ramifications.

According to the official faith of "Hislam," some verses of the Quran abrogate other verses, and even some hadith abrogate some verses as supported by distortion of the meaning of this verse. The Quran has a peculiar language. The singular word "Ayah" occurs 84 times in the Quran, and nowhere it is used for the verses of the Quran; rather, it is always used to mean "sign, evidence, or miracle." However, the plural form of this word, "Ayaat," is additionally used for verses of the Quran. The fact that a verse of the Quran does not demonstrate the miraculous characteristics of the Quran supports this peculiar usage of the word. For instance, short verses existed that were comprised of only one or two words, and they were most likely used in frequent daily conversations, letters, and poetry. For example, see: 55:3; 69:1; 74;4; 75:8; 80:28; 81:26. Furthermore, we are informed that the minimum unit demonstrating Quran's miraculous nature is a chapter (10:38) and the shortest chapter consists of 3 verses (103; 108, 110). The first verse of the Quran, commonly known as Basmala, cannot be a miracle on his own, but it gains a miraculous nature with its numerical network with other letters, words, verses, and chapters of the Quran. By not using the singular form "Ayah" for the verses of the Quran, God made it possible to distinguish the miracles shown in the text and prophecies of the scripture from the miracles shown in nature. See 4:82 for further evidence that the Quranic verses do not abrogate each other.

QUESTION 6: Was Pharaoh killed or not killed by drowning?

1. "We took the Children of Israel across the sea: Pharaoh and his hosts followed them in insolence and spite. At length, when overwhelmed with the flood, he said: 'I believe that there is no god except Him Whom the Children of Israel believe in: I am of those who submit (to Allah in Islam).' (It was said to him): 'Ah now!- But a little while before, wast thou in rebellion!- and thou didst mischief (and violence)! This day shall We save thee in the body, that thou mayest be a sign to those who come after thee!' But verily, many among mankind are heedless of Our Signs!" (10:90-92).

2. "Moses said, 'Thou knowest well that these things have been sent down by none but the Lord of the heavens and the earth as eye-opening evidence: and I consider thee indeed, O Pharaoh, to be one doomed to destruction!' So he resolved to remove them from the face of the earth: but We did drown him and all who were with him," (17:102-103).

ANSWER 6: Pharaoh was killed by drowning and his body was saved via mummification.

Verse 10:92 does not say that God will keep Pharaoh alive; it informs us that God will preserve his body after drowning him.

QUESTION 7 Is wine consumption good or bad?

1. "O ye who believe! Intoxicants and gambling, (dedication of) stones, and (divination by) arrows, are an abomination,- of Satan's handwork: eschew such (abomination), that ye may prosper," (5:90).

2. "(Here is) a Parable of the Garden which the righteous are promised: in it are rivers of water incorruptible; rivers of milk of which the taste never changes; rivers of wine, a joy to those who drink; and rivers of honey pure and clear. In it there are for them all kinds of fruits; and Grace from their Lord. (Can those in such Bliss) be compared to such as shall dwell for ever in the Fire, and be given, to drink, boiling water, so that it cuts up their bowels (to pieces)?" (47:15).

3. "Truly the Righteous will be in Bliss: On Thrones (of Dignity) will they command a sight (of all things): Thou wilt recognize in their faces the beaming brightness of Bliss. Their thirst will be slaked with Pure Wine sealed," (83:22-25).

ANSWER 7: Consumption of wine is bad in this world.

The Quran strongly rebukes the consumption of intoxicants for believers. This is not an enforced legal prohibition; but left for individuals to decide. The reason for this prohibition is obvious: intoxicants, though may provide some social or psychological benefits to the consumer, impair judgment and intelligence and cause too many problems for the individual and for society. The Quran prohibits intoxicants to individuals due to various moral reasons (the designer and creator of your body and mind asks you not to intentionally harm the body lent to you for a lifetime), intellectual reasons (the greatest gift you have is your brain and its power to make good judgments, so do not choose to be stupid or stupider than already you are) and pragmatic reasons (you and your society will suffer grave loss of health, wealth, happiness, and many lives, so do not contribute to the production and acceleration of such a destructive boomerang).

This said, let me suggest a correction. The verses 83:22-25 does not mention wine; thus, the translation is erroneous. The only verse that uses intoxicants (KHAMR) in a positive context is 47:15, and interestingly it is about paradise, or the hereafter. A quick reflection on the reason for prohibition of intoxicants explains the apparent contradiction. Harm from intoxicants, such as drunk driving, domestic violence or alcoholism, may not occur in another universe where the laws and rules are different. In other words, a person rewarded by eternal paradise will not hurt himself or herself or anyone else through intoxication (See 7:43; 15:47; 21:102; 41:31; 43:71; 2:112; 5:69).

QUESTION 8: Has the Quran been abrogated?

No, the Quran is perfect and can never be abrogated. However, some verses have been abrogated.

"There is none to alter the decisions of Allah." (6:34).

"Perfected is the Word of thy Lord in truth and justice. There is naught that can change His words." (6:115).

"There is no changing the Words of Allah." (10:64).

"And recite that which hath been revealed unto thee of the Scripture of thy Lord. There is none who can change His words." (18:27).

Yes, some verses have been abrogated.

"And when We put a revelation in place of (another) revelation, - and Allah knoweth best what He revealeth - they say: Lo! thou art but inventing. Most of them know not." (16:101).

"Nothing of our revelation (even a single verse) do we abrogate or cause be forgotten, but we bring (in place) one better or the like thereof." (2:106).

ANSWER 8: No, there is no abrogation in the Quran.

This question received its answer when I answered Question 5 above.

QUESTION 9: Who chooses the devils to be friends of disbelievers?

Allah?

"We have made the devils protecting friends for those who believe not." (7:27).

Or the disbelievers?

"A party hath He led aright, while error hath just hold over (another) party, for lo! they choose the devils for protecting supporters instead of Allah and deem that they are rightly guided." (7:30).

ANSWER 9: Disbelievers choose evil and devils in accordance to God's law which tests us on this planet.

While the Quran states that every event happens in accordance to God's design and permission (8:17; 57:22-25), the Quran also informs us regarding our freedom to choose our path (6:110;13:11; 18:29 42:13,48; 46:15).

QUESTION 10: Will all Jews and Christians go to hell?

Yes, all Christians will go to hell.

"Whoso seeketh as religion other than the Surrender (to Allah) it will not be accepted from him, and he will be a loser in the Hereafter." (3:85).

"They surely disbelieve who say: Lo! Allah is the Messiah, son of Mary. ... Lo! whoso ascribeth partners unto Allah, for him Allah hath forbidden paradise. His abode is the Fire. For evil-doers there will be no helpers." (5:72).

No, some will not.

"Those who are Jews, and Christians, and Sabaeans - whoever believeth in Allah and the Last Day and doeth right - surely their reward is with their Lord, and there shall no fear come upon them neither shall they grieve. (2:62).

"Lo! those who believe, and those who are Jews, and Sabaeans, and Christians - Whosoever believeth in Allah and the Last Day and doeth right - there shall no fear come upon them neither shall they grieve." (5:69).

ANSWER 10: Some Jews and Christians will go to hell.

First, the Quran terms the followers of Jesus using the word Nazarenes. Second, the word Sabaean is not a proper name referring to a particular religion. Rather, it is a verb meaning "those who are from other religions."

The critic assumes that surrender to God is only possible if someone utters a magical Arabic word. Islam is not a proper name, neither did it start with Muhammad, nor did it end with Muhammad. Any person who dedicates himself or herself to God alone, believes in the day of judgment, and lives a righteous life — regardless of the name of their religion — is considered muslim. There are many people among Christians and Jews who fit this description.

Brainbow Press

Quran: A Reformist Translation
   Translated and Annotated by: Edip Yuksel; Layth Saleh al-Shaiban; Martha
   Schulte-Nafeh. First Edition: Brainbow Press, 2007, 520 pages, $24.70.
   ISBN 978-0-9796715-0-0. Available also in **pocket size**.

Test Your Quranic Knowledge
   Contains six sets of multiple choice questions and their answers. Edip Yuksel,
   Brainbow Press, 2007, 88 pages, $7.95. ISBN 978-0-9796715-5-5

Manifesto for Islamic Reform
   Edip Yuksel, Brainbow Press, 2008, 209, 128 pages, $9.95.
   ISBN 978-0-9796715-6-2

The Natural Republic
   Layth Saleh al-Shaiban (ProgressiveMuslims.org), Brainbow Press, 2008, 198
   pages, $14.95, ISBN 978-0-9796715-8-6

Critical Thinkers for Islamic Reform
   Editors: Edip Yuksel, Arnold Mol, Farouk A. Peru, Brainbow Press, 2009, 262
   pages, $17.95. ISBN 978-0-9796715-7-9

NINETEEN: God's Signature in Nature and Scripture
   A comprehensive demonstration of the prophetic miracle. Edip Yuksel, Brainbow
   Press, 2010, 456 pages. $19.95. ISBN 978-0-9796715-3-1

Peacemaker's Guide to Warmongers
   Exposing Robert Spencer, Osama bin Laden, David Horowitz, Mullah Omar, Bill
   Warner, Ali Sina and other Enemies of Peace. Edip Yuksel, Brainbowpress, 2010,
   432 pages. $19.95. ISBN: 978-0-9796715-3-1

Edip Yuksel's Upcoming Books in years 2010-2014

My Journey from Sunni Religion to Islam (Provisional Title)
   An autobiography.

Running Like Zebras
   Edip Yüksel's debate with the critics of Code 19

19 Questions for Muslims, Christians, and Atheists
   The first two sections are revisions of old booklets.

Purple Letters
   A selection of correspondence on religion, philosophy, and politics.

From Blind Faith to Rational Monotheism: Inspiring Stories of Forty Converts
   Inspiring stories of converts from Sunni, Shiite, Catholic, Protestant religions and
   Atheism to Islam.

The Bestest Teacher, Student and Parent:
   57 Rules for Students, Teachers and Parents.

Twelve Hungry Men
   A religious/political/philosophical comedy for a feature film

Edip's Record of Religious Oddities:
   A ranking of the bizarre beliefs and practices of world religions.

USA versus USA: The American Janus
   A political mirror and x-ray of America's best and worst.

Muhammad: A Messenger of Peace and Reason
   A script for an animated feature film about Muhammad's mission.

Join the Movement; Let the World Know!

The Islamic Reform movement is receiving momentum around the globe. We invite you to join us in our activities locally, internationally. Please contact us through the contact addresses posted at:

www.islamicreform.org
www.free-minds.org
www.mpjp.org
www.19.org

To study the Quran more diligently, you may visit 19.org for links to computer programs, searchable Quranic indexes, electronic versions of this and other translations, and various study tools. We highly recommend you the following sites for your study of the Quran:

www.quranic.org
www.quranix.com
www.openquran.org
www.studyquran.org
www.quranmiracles.org
www.quranconnection.com

****

www.19.org
www.yuksel.org
www.quranix.com
www.studyquran.org
www.quranbrowser.com
www.brainbowpress.com
www.quranconnection.com
www.groups.google.com/group/19org
www.deenresearchcenter.com
www.islamicreform.org
www.quranmiracles.org
www.openburhan.com
www.free-minds.org
www.quranic.org
www.mpjp.org

…and more

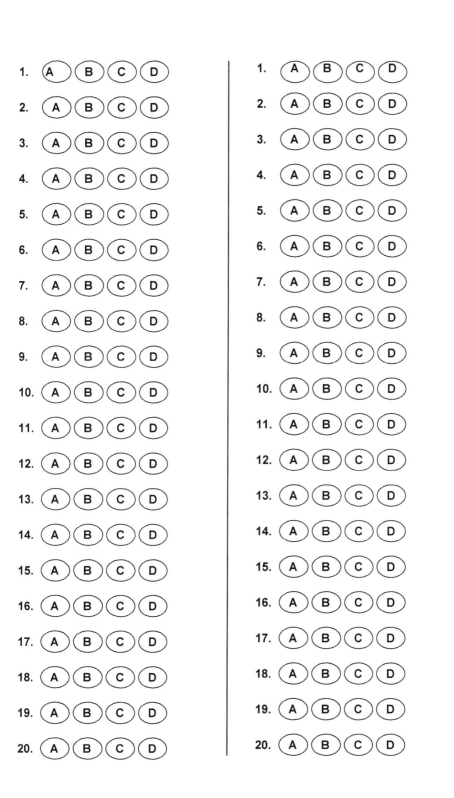

1.	A	B	C	D		1.	A	B	C	D
2.	A	B	C	D		2.	A	B	C	D
3.	A	B	C	D		3.	A	B	C	D
4.	A	B	C	D		4.	A	B	C	D
5.	A	B	C	D		5.	A	B	C	D
6.	A	B	C	D		6.	A	B	C	D
7.	A	B	C	D		7.	A	B	C	D
8.	A	B	C	D		8.	A	B	C	D
9.	A	B	C	D		9.	A	B	C	D
10.	A	B	C	D		10.	A	B	C	D
11.	A	B	C	D		11.	A	B	C	D
12.	A	B	C	D		12.	A	B	C	D
13.	A	B	C	D		13.	A	B	C	D
14.	A	B	C	D		14.	A	B	C	D
15.	A	B	C	D		15.	A	B	C	D
16.	A	B	C	D		16.	A	B	C	D
17.	A	B	C	D		17.	A	B	C	D
18.	A	B	C	D		18.	A	B	C	D
19.	A	B	C	D		19.	A	B	C	D
20.	A	B	C	D		20.	A	B	C	D

1. Ⓐ Ⓑ Ⓒ Ⓓ		1. Ⓐ Ⓑ Ⓒ Ⓓ
2. Ⓐ Ⓑ Ⓒ Ⓓ		2. Ⓐ Ⓑ Ⓒ Ⓓ
3. Ⓐ Ⓑ Ⓒ Ⓓ		3. Ⓐ Ⓑ Ⓒ Ⓓ
4. Ⓐ Ⓑ Ⓒ Ⓓ		4. Ⓐ Ⓑ Ⓒ Ⓓ
5. Ⓐ Ⓑ Ⓒ Ⓓ		5. Ⓐ Ⓑ Ⓒ Ⓓ
6. Ⓐ Ⓑ Ⓒ Ⓓ		6. Ⓐ Ⓑ Ⓒ Ⓓ
7. Ⓐ Ⓑ Ⓒ Ⓓ		7. Ⓐ Ⓑ Ⓒ Ⓓ
8. Ⓐ Ⓑ Ⓒ Ⓓ		8. Ⓐ Ⓑ Ⓒ Ⓓ
9. Ⓐ Ⓑ Ⓒ Ⓓ		9. Ⓐ Ⓑ Ⓒ Ⓓ
10. Ⓐ Ⓑ Ⓒ Ⓓ		10. Ⓐ Ⓑ Ⓒ Ⓓ
11. Ⓐ Ⓑ Ⓒ Ⓓ		11. Ⓐ Ⓑ Ⓒ Ⓓ
12. Ⓐ Ⓑ Ⓒ Ⓓ		12. Ⓐ Ⓑ Ⓒ Ⓓ
13. Ⓐ Ⓑ Ⓒ Ⓓ		13. Ⓐ Ⓑ Ⓒ Ⓓ
14. Ⓐ Ⓑ Ⓒ Ⓓ		14. Ⓐ Ⓑ Ⓒ Ⓓ
15. Ⓐ Ⓑ Ⓒ Ⓓ		15. Ⓐ Ⓑ Ⓒ Ⓓ
16. Ⓐ Ⓑ Ⓒ Ⓓ		16. Ⓐ Ⓑ Ⓒ Ⓓ
17. Ⓐ Ⓑ Ⓒ Ⓓ		17. Ⓐ Ⓑ Ⓒ Ⓓ
18. Ⓐ Ⓑ Ⓒ Ⓓ		18. Ⓐ Ⓑ Ⓒ Ⓓ
19. Ⓐ Ⓑ Ⓒ Ⓓ		19. Ⓐ Ⓑ Ⓒ Ⓓ
20. Ⓐ Ⓑ Ⓒ Ⓓ		20. Ⓐ Ⓑ Ⓒ Ⓓ

1.	A B C D			1.	A B C D		
2.	A B C D			2.	A B C D		
3.	A B C D			3.	A B C D		
4.	A B C D			4.	A B C D		
5.	A B C D			5.	A B C D		
6.	A B C D			6.	A B C D		
7.	A B C D			7.	A B C D		
8.	A B C D			8.	A B C D		
9.	A B C D			9.	A B C D		
10.	A B C D			10.	A B C D		
11.	A B C D			11.	A B C D		
12.	A B C D			12.	A B C D		
13.	A B C D			13.	A B C D		
14.	A B C D			14.	A B C D		
15.	A B C D			15.	A B C D		
16.	A B C D			16.	A B C D		
17.	A B C D			17.	A B C D		
18.	A B C D			18.	A B C D		
19.	A B C D			19.	A B C D		
20.	A B C D			20.	A B C D		

21. (A) (B) (C) (D)
22. (A) (B) (C) (D)
23. (A) (B) (C) (D)
24. (A) (B) (C) (D)
25. (A) (B) (C) (D)
26. (A) (B) (C) (D)
27. (A) (B) (C) (D)
28. (A) (B) (C) (D)
29. (A) (B) (C) (D)
30. (A) (B) (C) (D)
31. (A) (B) (C) (D)
32. (A) (B) (C) (D)
33. (A) (B) (C) (D)
34. (A) (B) (C) (D)
35. (A) (B) (C) (D)
36. (A) (B) (C) (D)
37. (A) (B) (C) (D)
38. (A) (B) (C) (D)
39. (A) (B) (C) (D)
40. (A) (B) (C) (D)

21. (A) (B) (C) (D)
22. (A) (B) (C) (D)
23. (A) (B) (C) (D)
24. (A) (B) (C) (D)
25. (A) (B) (C) (D)
26. (A) (B) (C) (D)
27. (A) (B) (C) (D)
28. (A) (B) (C) (D)
29. (A) (B) (C) (D)
30. (A) (B) (C) (D)
31. (A) (B) (C) (D)
32. (A) (B) (C) (D)
33. (A) (B) (C) (D)
34. (A) (B) (C) (D)
35. (A) (B) (C) (D)
36. (A) (B) (C) (D)
37. (A) (B) (C) (D)
38. (A) (B) (C) (D)
39. (A) (B) (C) (D)
40. (A) (B) (C) (D)

CPSIA information can be obtained
at www.ICGtesting.com
Printed in the USA
BVHW07s1440040918
526489BV00001B/15/P

9 780979 671555